Thinking Like A

ROMANCE WRITER

The Sensual Writer's Sourcebook of Words and Phrases

DAHLIA EVANS

Copyright Notice

Published By:
Satin Publishing

Copyright © 2013 by Dahlia Evans. All Rights Reserved.

No part of this publication may be replicated, redistributed, or given away in any form without the prior written consent of the publisher.

ISBN-10:
1499760108

ISBN-13:
978-1499760101

For Mum

Contents

Introduction   *1*

PART I: Describing the Body

1. Hair   *5*
2. Head   *8*
3. Face   *10*
4. Eyes   *12*
5. Nose   *16*
6. Mouth   *18*
7. Tongue   *20*
8. Teeth   *22*
9. Lips   *24*
10. Jaw   *26*
11. Neck   *28*
12. Shoulders   *30*
13. Chest   *32*
14. Breasts   *34*
15. Nipples   *36*
16. Heart   *38*
17. Arms   *40*
18. Hands   *42*
19. Fingers   *44*
20. Back   *46*
21. Bottom   *48*
22. Abdomen / Stomach   *50*
23. Hips / Waist   *52*
24. Penis   *54*
25. Vulva / Vagina   *57*
26. Thighs   *60*
27. Legs   *62*
28. Feet   *64*
29. Body   *66*
30. Skin   *68*

PART II: Describing Senses and Emotions

31. Senses　　　　　　*73*
32. Feelings　　　　　 *77*
33. Facial Expressions　　*81*

PART III: Describing Intimacy

34. Voice　　　　*87*
35. Breathing　　*90*
36. Kissing　　　*92*
37. Sex　　　　　*94*

Introduction

It may surprise you to discover that all of the biggest and bestselling romance authors over the last 25 years have been guarding a secret that once revealed will give any writer the ability to create sexy stories that read like a bestseller.

And here's the secret...

Most romance writers use the same descriptive words and phrases. That's right!

When I first discovered this fact I couldn't believe it. But again and again the same words and phrases kept popping up in different books by different authors. Were these authors plagiarizing each other, I wondered? Or instead was it simply a matter of there being a limited amount of words that could be used to describe particular body parts or actions?

Whatever the reason, I was determined to compile these words and phrases. So I spent the better part of four months reading through hundreds of romance novels, sifting through each and every one, looking for choice words and phrases. The result is a romance thesaurus unlike anything ever seen before.

Thinking Like A Romance Writer contains 37 categories with over 8,500 words and phrases that have been used in romance novels time and time again to describe every intimate encounter imaginable.

How This Book Is Organized

1. Each category is broken up into sections (root words; adjectives, verbs, descriptive combinations; descriptive phrases).

2. Entries are sorted alphabetically.

3. Each entry is separated by a semicolon or line break.

You will notice that some categories are more detailed than others. This is due to the fact that certain details, such as teeth, are rarely described in a novel - perhaps two or three times if that. Whereas other details, like eyes, are used much more to convey emotions and intentions. In sections such is this, you will find an abundance of useful words and phrases that will help make your prose sparkle.

If you intend on writing traditional romance novels, then you will find the sections dealing with genitalia unnecessary. However, those of you interesting in writing erotic romance, or pure erotica, those sections will give you a treasure-trove of descriptors for crafting intimate love scenes.

How to Use This Book

This book is best used as a thesaurus for your romance writing projects. So for example, let's say you are writing a scene that involves the hero's hands touching the heroine's body. You can go to the category titled 'Hands' and find the necessary words to help you construct descriptive sentences.

- *Does your hero have strong hands?* Perhaps a descriptive adjective like 'powerful' could be used.

- *Are you not sure what action a hand can make?* Look under the 'Verbs - Things A Hand Can Do' section. Perhaps 'brushed over' is a fit for your scene.

- *Are you struggling with sentence ideas?* Look over the 'Descriptive Phrases' for inspiration in constructing your own sentences.

Finally, I want to thank you for your investment. I hope this resource helps ignite your creativity.

Warm Wishes,
Dahlia Evans

PART I:
Describing the Body

1
Words and Phrases to Describe Hair

Colors

ash-blond; auburn; black; blonde/blond; buttermilk blonde; dark brown; gray; iron-gray; light brown; medium brown; red; salt and pepper; white; wine-red.

Styles

afro; bangs; beehive; bob cut; bouffant; bowl cut; braid; bun; butch; buzz cut; chignon; chonmage; comb over; cornrows; crew cut; crop; crown braid; devilock; dreadlocks; ducktail; Dutch braid; emo; fauxhawk; finger wave; fishtail; flattop; flip; fontange; French twist; fringe; frosted tips; hi-top fade; highlights; hime cut; ivy league; liberty spikes; mohawk; mop-top; mullet; odengo; pageboy; part; payot; perm; pigtail; plait; pompadour; ponytail; rats tail; ringlet; undercut; up-do; waves.

Adjectives

aging; blow-dried; bobbed; bright; bristly; bushy; close-cropped; coiffed; coiffured; colorful; coppery; crinkly; curly; curtained; damp; dark; disheveled; drab; dry; fair; fairy; feathered; flowing; flyaway; frizzy; frosted; fuzzy; glorious; glossy; gorgeous; greasy; grizzled; healthy-looking; lanky; light; long; loose; luxuriant; maintained; matted; medium-length; messy; moonlight-pale; natural; neatly combed; neglected;

no-nonsense; oily; pale; parted; plain; pretty; ruffled; rumpled; scraggly; scruffy; shaggy; shiny; short; shoulder-length; silken; silky; sleek; slicked back; slovenly; spiky; splitting; straight; styled; sunbeam; swept-back; tangled; tawny; thick; thin; thinning; tidy; tousled; trimmed; uncombed; unhealthy-looking; unkempt; unnatural; untidy; vivid; wavy; well-kept; wet; wild; wind-blown; windswept; wiry; wispy.

Descriptive Combinations

dark-haired; fall of hair; furrow of hair; grizzled gray hair; hair flowing in loose spiral curls; mane of hair; spiky shock of hair; sprinkled with whorls of hair; stray strand of hair; tangle of hair; tumbled fall of hair; wildly tousled hair.

Verbs – Things Hair Can Do

blew; blew back; bounced; bounced against; bounced on; drooped over; feathered around; fell; fell back; flamed around; flying across; glinted; lay in a tangle; peppered; pool; rippled across; shone; slid across; spilled forward; spilled off the edge; spread around; strayed; stretched; tumbled around; waved; waved around.

Verbs – Things That Can Be Done to Hair

brushed; brushed back; burnished; clipped back; delved into; dried; dried off; fixed; grabbed; knotted; mussed; plowed through; plunged into; pushed behind; pushed off; raked back; raked through; ruffled; scraped back; sliced through; smoothed back; smoothed over; stroked; swathed; tackled; tied circumspectly back; touched; tousled; unraveled; wet; wound.

Descriptive Phrases

He had brilliant blue eyes, short blonde hair, and a chiseled jaw that made her swoon.

He reached out and tucked a strand of hair behind his ear.

His shoulder-length hair spilled over his face.

She raked her hand through his silky dark hair.

She reached up to fix her windswept hair.

She sighed and raked her hand through her hair.

2
Words and Phrases to Describe the Head

Adjectives

aching; arrogant; auburn; blonde; bright; clear; curly; dark; domed; good; handsome; heavy; imperious; little; pale; pounding; pretty; proud; tousled; ugly; unhelpful; well-shaped; woozy.

Descriptive Combinations

beat her head against a wall; crown of her head; curly brown head; dark curly head; fair head; head over heels; inside his head; lost his head; thoughts swimming around in his head.

Verbs – Things a Head Can Do

ached; angled; banged against; bent; bobbed; bowed; bumped; cleared; cocked; dragged; dropped; dropped back; ducked; fell back; filled; flew up; flung back; held high; knew; leaned on; lifted; lolled back; lolled sideways; moved; nodded; poked out; poked over; pressed against; raised; reared; rested; rested against; rocked back; shifted; shook; spun around; stuck around; stuck inside; sunk into; swam; swiveled; threw back; tilted; tipped; tipped forward; tossed back; tucked beneath; turned; twisted around.

Verbs – Things That Can Be Done to a Head

caressed; clouded; clubbed; elbowed; hit; kissed; messed with; pinned; pressed; rubbed; scratched; slapped; slid over; smacked across; touched; tugged back; wrapped; yanked over.

Descriptive Phrases

He couldn't deny it any longer; he was head over heels in love with her.

He turned his head away from her piercing stare.

She shook her head in disbelief.

She threw her head back, tears rolling down her cheeks.

She tilted her head to one side, studying the expression on his face.

3
Words and Phrases to Describe the Face

Root Words

brow; cheek; cheekbone; chin; face; features; forehead.

Adjectives

aged; aging; airy; angelic; angry; angular; aristocratic; arresting; astute; beautiful; bleached; bleak; bony; bright red; brooding; calculating; carved; child-like; chiseled; chubby; cold; dark; delicate; desolate; divine; drawn; dreamy; eager; emaciated; emotionless; feminine; flushed; gaunt; gorgeous; gray; grim; haggard; handsome; happy; hard; hardened; high; horrified; icy; imperious; jealous; jowly; lined; little; long; low; marble; masculine; narrow; nonchalant; old; pale; perfect; pointy; porcelain; precious; pure; rough; sad; sinister; smooth; steely; striking; stunning; sullen; thin; ugly; unassuming; warm; wide; wrinkled.

Descriptive Combinations

dark, brooding features; face of an angel; face to face; hard and handsome face; high, chiseled cheekbones; marble cheekbones; pallor of her face; thrown back in her face; two-faced.

Verbs – Things the Face Can Do

appeared; betrayed; blood drained from; blushed; boiled; burned; changed; contorted; darkened; darkened with frustration; deadpan look on; desperation showed on; drained of color; expectant look on; faced; felt get hot; felt heat creep into; felt tears against; forced a smile; frowned; grim expression on; haunted; haunted expression on; imperious look on; kept neutral; knowing look on; lightened; look of stubbornness on; lowered; mutinous expression on; pulsed; raised; screwed up; shuttered expression on; smile fixed to; stunned look on; tensed; tilted down; tilted to the left; tilted to the right; tilted up; tried to compose; truculent expression on; turned red; went slightly pale; willed to remain calm.

Verbs – Things That Can Be Done to the Face

applied foundation to; approached; breath felt warm against; caught chin between thumb and forefinger; covered; dried; explored the contours of; fixed; focused on; gazed upon; gently massaged; hid; hit; infatuated by; kissed; licked; looked down at; loved; mesmerized by; met; pinched; punched; put makeup on; ran hand down; rubbed; saw the look on; scratched; scrubbed; shaved; shoved in; slapped across; slid down; smeared; smoothed over; smothered; squeezed; stared into; struck; studied; surveyed; tilted up; touched; washed; wet; wiped; wiped makeup from.

Descriptive Phrases

As his eyes studied her, she hoped her face didn't betray the hurt she felt inside.

Her face was set in a hard, determined expression.

He touched her face and gently wiped away her tears.

She saw his face go slightly pale.

She stared down at him, with an expectant look on her face.

4
Words and Phrases to Describe Eyes

Root Words

awareness; eyes; focus; gaze; glance; perception; stare; vision.

Eye Colors

amber; black; blue; brown; gray; green; hazel; violet.

Green Variations

bottle green; Caribbean green; chartreuse; dark pastel green; earls green; emerald green; erinite; forest green; grass green; jade green; khaki; leaf green; olive; olivine; opal green; opaline green; sea green.

Blue Variations

aqua; aquamarine; Arctic blue; Atlantic blue; azure; baby blue; Bondi blue; bright indigo; capri; cerulean; cobalt blue; cornflower blue; crystal blue; cyan; dark azure; dark blue; dark powder blue; deep azure; denim blue; electric blue; electric ultramarine; gunmetal blue; ice blue; indigo; lavender; light blue; light cornflower; light cyan; medium navy blue; midnight blue; navy blue; periwinkle; Persian blue; powder blue; Prussian blue; royal blue; sapphire; sky blue; slate blue; steel blue; steel blue; turquoise; ultramarine.

Brown/Amber Variations

autumn; bistre; brandy; bronze; cafe noir; champagne; chestnut; chocolate; cognac; copper; fiery; golden; honey; nut brown; russet; rustic; saddle brown; sandalwood; sepia; sienna; sugar brown; sunset; topaz; walnut; whiskey.

Violet Variations

amethyst; hyacinth; imperial violet; indigo; lavender; magenta; rose violet.

Black Variations

anthracite; black olive; coal black; ebony; jet; obsidian; pitch black; smoky; soot.

Gray Variations

charcoal gray; cloud gray; dark gray; dark slate gray; dim gray; graphite; gray; gunmetal; light gray; light slate gray; silver; slate gray; smoky; steel.

Adjectives

adorable; adventurous; aggressive; amorous; angry; anxious; appraising; ardent; arrogant; artless; assessing; attentive; attractive; beady; beautiful; bewildered; bloodshot; bored; bright; brilliant; bug-eyed; burning; busy; cautious; clear; cloudy; cold; compelling; concerned; confused; contemplative; crazy; creepy; cruel; curious; cute; dancing; dangerous; dark; darting; dead; deep; deep-set; defiant; determined; devilish; disapproving; discerning; distinct; doe-eyed; doubtful; dreamy; dull; dynamic; eager; earnest; enchanting; enthusiastic; enticing; envious; evil; exotic; extraordinary; fervent; fierce; flashing; flat; frantic; furtive; gentle; glamorous; gleaming; glinting; glistening; glittering; gloomy; greedy; hard; haughty; heavy; hollow; hooded; hungry; innocent; inquiring; inquisitive; insolent; intelligent; intense; intent; jealous; judgmental; keen; kind; lady-killer; large; lascivious; lazy; lecherous; lidded; liquid; lonely; longing;

lovely; lust-filled; lustful; magnetic; mischievous; misty; motionless; mysterious; narrow; naughty; obedient; oval-shaped; over-zealous; pale; passionate; passionless; passive; powerful; pretty; protuberant; proud; prying; radiant; remote; rheumy; riveting; round; sad; savage; scandalous; scrutinizing; searching; serene; sexy; sharp; shuttered; shy; sin-filled; sinful; sleepy; sly; small; smiling; smoldering; soulful; soulless; sparkling; stealthy; stony; stormy; suggestive; sullen; sunken; tantalizing; teary; tired; treacherous; troubled; twinkling; unfathomable; unspeaking; vast; vivacious; wanton; warm; watchful; weary; wicked; wide; wild; worried; worrisome; zealous.

Descriptive Combinations

cold, hungry eyes; dark, deep eyes; deep brown eyes; devilishly defiant eyes; fiery cooper eyes; greedy green eyes; raw, hungry eyes; rustic honey eyes; smoky black eyes; sparkling silver eyes.

Verbs – Things Eyes Can Do

adjusted; admired; appraised; assayed; averted; bathed; beheld; betrayed; blazed; blazed down; blinked; browsed; captured; caressed; cast a glance; caught sight of; checked; checked out; closed; darkened; darted; descried; detected; discovered; diverted; drank in; drank up; dropped; envisaged; envisioned; espied; examined; eyeballed; eyed; faced; fixed; fixed eyes on; flashed; flickered; focused; followed; froze; gawked; gazed; gazed upon; glanced; glared; glazed; gleamed; glimpsed; glinted; gloated; goggled; grew wild; hardened; identified; impaled; inspected; looked; lowered; made eyes at; made out; marked; marveled; melted into; met; monitored; narrowed; noted; noticed; observed; ogled; opened; overlooked; oversaw; passed over; peeked; peeped; peered; perceived; pierced; pored over; pried; probed; raised; read; recognized; reflected; regarded; registered; relaxed; riveted; roamed; rolled; roved over; saw; scanned; scoped out; scoured; scrutinized; searched; seared into; set eyes on; sharpened; shut; sifted; sighted; sized up; skimmed; skirted; snooped; sought; sparkled; spied; spotted; squinted; stared; studied; supervised; surveyed; swept over; tended; took note of; traced; twinkled; undressed; viewed; visualized; watched; widened; winked; witnessed.

Descriptive Phrases

He appraised her curvaceous figure.

Her eyes glazed with need.

His cold hungry eyes peered through the darkness.

She ran her fingers down his bulging chest watching his wicked eyes urge her further.

She took a cursory glance at his magnificent bulge.

5
Words and Phrases to Describe the Nose

Adjectives

aesthetic; angular; appealing; Aquiline; aristocratic; arrogant; attractive; beak-like; beaky; bent; big; bold; bony; bowed; broad; bulbous; button-like; cherry-colored; chiseled; classic; concave; convex; crooked; curved; cute; dainty; defined; delicate; diminutive; distended; distinctive; enormous; feminine; flat; freckled; godly; graceful; Grecian; handsome; hard; harsh; hawkish; honest; hooked; immaculate; infallible; keen; large; lengthy; little; masculine; narrow; narrow-bladed; narrow-bridged; peppered; perfect; pert; petite; plain; pointy; pretty; prominent; protruding; protuberant; proud; puffy; red; Roman; Romanesque; rounded; runny; sculpted; shapely; simple; small; straight; striking; strong; subtle; superior; swollen; thin; trim; turned-up; upturned; well-shaped.

Descriptive Combinations

aesthetically pleasing nose; aristocratic jut of his nose; arrogant blade of a nose; arrogant jut of his classic nose; arrogant masculine nose; dainty little nose; delicate little nose; endearingly freckled nose; infallible perfection of his nose; light sprinkling of freckles over her nose; perfectly formed nose; pink tip of her nose; right under her nose; slightly prominent nose; slightly turned-up nose; small, pert nose; straight, proud nose; straight classic nose; strong, rounded nose; superior little nose of hers; unrepentantly upturned nose.

Verbs – Things a Nose Can Do

blew; buried in; danced over; danced with; dug into; gave warning; leaned against; looked down; nosedived; nuzzled; pressed against; pressed to; skirted across; skirted over; smooth over; stuck in the air; turned up; turned up at the tip; twitched; wrinkled.

Verbs - Things That Can Be Done to a Nose

admired; anchored on; attached to; blew; cut off; dangled under; kissed; latched onto; licked; pecked; picked; ran fingers along; replaced on; rubbed; took; traced; wiped.

Descriptive Phrases

He lightly kissed her perfectly formed nose.

She licked the tip of his slightly prominent nose.

She loved everything about his face; from his brown eyes to his roman nose.

She raised her dainty little nose in defiance.

That arrogant masculine nose made her want him even more.

6
Words and Phrases to Describe the Mouth

Adjectives

addictive; alluring; ardent; arrogant; attractive; bad-mouthed; beautiful; big; bitter; carnal; chiseled; cold; cynical; delicious; dreamy; dry; eloquent; expressive; feminine; firm; full; gorgeous; handsome; hot; hungry; incredible; knowing; large; little; luscious; lush; masculine; mobile; moist; passionate; petite; pompous; potty-mouthed; pretty; pretty; ripe; salacious; satiny; scornful; sensual; sensuous; sexy; sinful; small; smart-mouthed; soft; swollen; vengeful; warm; wet; wicked; wide-mouthed; willing.

Descriptive Combinations

carnal, sensuous mouth; chiseled, sensuous mouth; chiseled lines of his mouth; curve to her soft mouth; desire curving her mouth; down-curve of her mouth; full, sexy mouth; lush sweetness of her mouth; melt in the mouth; mouth compressed to a hard line; mouths hanging open; salacious grin; satiny softness of her mouth; sinfully beautiful mouth; stern, sensuous mouth; strained line of his sculpted mouth; sweet depths of her mouth; tantalizing proximity of his mouth; tender interior of her mouth; tightly closed mouth; warm and willing mouth; wickedly sensual mouth.

Verbs – Things the Mouth Can Do

anchored to; angled; angled under; breathed through; brought back; burst open; came down on; closed; compressed; covered scream with; curled;

curved; curved up; demanded; drew into; dried; dropped open; edged up at the corners; edged up in a half smile; faintly smiled; fell open; fitted over; forced onto; gaped; gasped; gasped for air; grimaced; grinned; groaned; hardened; held a smile; hung open; kissed; latched on; laughed; loosened; mouthed; moved; opened; pressed against; pressed to; protested; quirked at the corners; quivered; ran dry; relaxed; rubbed against; sealed shut; shut; skimmed; slanted; smiled; smile touched; smirked; sneered; softened; spit; stilled; sucked; suckled; surrendered; tightened; took into; toyed with; trembled; twisted; twisted with pain; twitched; watered; whimpered; wobbled; words fell from; words fell out of; words left; wrapped around; yearned.

Verbs – Things That Can Be Done to the Mouth

buck up into; captured in; claimed; covered; devoured; explored; eyes drifted to; eyes flicked to; eyes trained on; fingers moved to; found; gaze drifted to; gazed upon; groaned into; growled into; held palm up to; kissed on; plundered; plunged into; popped into; pressed against; pulled back from; punched; put a hand over; put fingers in; recaptured; resented; rubbed against; skimmed; slapped; slid in; slid inside; slid out; slipped tongue into; stared at; straddled; studied; sunk into; tasted; tongue thrust into; took possession of; traced the outline; wiped; yearned for.

Descriptive Phrases

Disgust twisted her pretty mouth into a sneer.

He devoured her mouth with deep sweeping strokes of his tongue.

He took hungry possession of her mouth.

His mouth tightened in a grimace.

His open mouth came down on hers.

She drew his tongue into her mouth.

7
Words and Phrases to Describe the Tongue

Adjectives

coiling; crimson; expert; extended; hot; long; magic; pointed; pointy; relentless; ruthless; satin-like; seductive; serpentine; silken; silky; skillful; slippery; spongy; tender; velvet; warm; wet.

Descriptive Combinations

coiling crimson tongue; expert touch of his tongue; length of his tongue; skillfully silky tongue; slippery satin tongue; soft, exploring tongue; velvet warmth of her tongue; wet serpentine tongue.

Verbs – Things a Tongue Can Do

assaulted; breached; brushed; brushed across; caressed; charted; circled; coiled; collided with; connected; consumed; curled; curled around; danced; darted; devoured; dipped between; discovered; dissected; dived deep; dragged; drew a path; drew into; elicited a moan; encircled; entered; enveloped; examined; explored; extended; flicked; focused on; forced; forged deep; found; headed down; inspected; jabbed; lapped; lashed; laved; mapped; moved; moved between; navigated; pillaged; plundered; plunged; poked; possessed; pressed flat against; probed; prodded; pushed; ran across; ran over; reached; rolled; rolled over; scraped; searched; seduced; settled on; skimmed; skimmed over; slid; stimulate; stroked; stuck out; studied; surged; surveyed; swept over; swirled; tasted; taunted; teased;

tended; thrust; tongued; took; touched; toyed; trailed; twined; twirled; twisted; uncovered; whisked; worked; worried; zeroed in on.

Verbs – Things That Can Be Done to a Tongue

bit; cupped; devoured; engulfed; enveloped; nibbled; pinched; pulled; slurped; squeezed; sucked.

Descriptive Phrases

He took her in his arms and kissed her, his tongue dipping in.

His tongue made wet trails over her puckered lips.

She opened her mouth across his, her soft tongue lashing his.

Their tongues danced as each of their bodies melted together in this sacred union.

Using the tip of her tongue, she made circular motions up and down his length.

8
Words and Phrases to Describe Teeth

Adjectives

bare; brilliant; broken; chattering; chipped; crooked; dazzling; even; front; gleaming; glittering; large; little; lying; neat; needle-sharp; perfect; polished; sharp; shattered; shiny; small; snapping; sparkling; stellar; strong; white; yellow.

Descriptive Combinations

flash of white teeth; lower teeth; sharp little teeth; skin of her teeth; sparkling white teeth; gleaming teeth; perfectly straight teeth; upper teeth.

Verbs – Things Teeth Can Do

ached; bit down; caught between; chattered; clenched; clinked together; dangled from; flew apart; flew together; gleamed; gnashed; grazed; grazed across; gritted; gritted together; ground; lied through; lit (his) face; nibbled; nipped; pinched; pulled; rattled; sank into; scraped; scraped over; set; snapped together; took between; tucked between; tugged; twirled between; worried at.

Verbs – Things That Can Be Done to Teeth

brushed; cleaned; clinked against; pulled; punched; scrubbed; shattered; smacked; smoothed over; tapped against.

Descriptive Phrases

Her lips parted, revealed a flash of white teeth.

Her teeth bit down hard on his tender flesh.

His sparkling white teeth showed through his beautiful smile.

She gritted her teeth together.

She slid her bottom lip between her teeth.

9
Words and Phrases to Describe Lips

Adjectives

alluring; anemic; beautiful; bloodless; blue; cracked; damp; down-turned; dry; eager; enticing; fat; firm; full; glistening; glossy; gorgeous; heaven-sent; heavenly; hot pink; hungry; hypnotic; irresistible; juicy; luscious; moist; pale; pallid; parched; petulant; pink; plum-colored; plump; pouty; pursed; red; ruby; salty; seductive; sensual; sexy; silky; sinful; smooth; soft; succulent; sulky; sullen; sweet; swollen; thick; thin; warm; wet; wide.

Descriptive Combinations

beautiful swollen lips; champagne-wet lips; edges of her lips; full bottom lip; lingering imprint of his lips; petulant sulky lips; small crease at the edge of her lips; soft pink lips; tingly bottom lip; wide smooth lips.

Verbs – Things Lips Can Do

advanced; buttoned; curled; curled around; drew back; edged closer; enticed; enveloped; escaped; hovered; kissed; moistened; opened up; parted; pecked; pecked at; pleasured; pouted; pressed against; protruded; puckered; pursed; quivered; rested upon; shot from; slid across; slid over; smothered; spilled from; surrounded; teased; thrust; thrust forward; tingled; touched; trembled; turned down; wet; widened; worked over; zipped.

Verbs – Things That Can Be Done to Lips

bit; brought to; captured; circled; enraptured; focused on; found; held a finger to; knew; licked; liked; nibbled; nipped at; possessed; ran finger across; ran thumb over; settled upon; sipped; squeezed together; sucked; sucked between; suckled; teased; took; touched; wiped; wiped across.

Descriptive Phrases

A small breathless whisper escaped her lips.

His sweet warm breath lingered just above her swollen lips.

His tongue dipped between the seam of her lips.

She glanced at his towel and licked her lips.

She instinctively curled her lips around his tongue.

10
Words and Phrases to Describe the Jaw

Root Words

jaw; jaw line; lower jaw; upper jaw.

Adjectives

aesthetic; aristocratic; arrogant; balanced; beautiful; broad; chiseled; curved; curvy; dark; delineated; elegant; feminine; formidable; hard; hearty; loose; masculine; muscular; noble; petite; pleasing; regal; rock-hard; roughened; rounded; shapely; slight; square; statuesque; straight; strong; stubble-marked; tense; think; tight; tough; uncompromising; well-formed; well-rounded.

Descriptive Combinations

aesthetic, well-formed jaw; angular curve of his jaw; dark stubble shadowed his jaw; five o'clock shadow; hard, angular jaw line; jaw clenched brutally tight; jaw clenched savagely; jaw line hard as a rock; jaw tightened in anger; jaw tightened with force; sharply angled jaw; the hard line of his jaw.

Verbs – Things the Jaw Can Do

ached; angled; clenched; closed; cracked; creaked; drooped; dropped;

flexed; hardened; jerked; leaned against; leaned on; loosened; muscle jumped in; muscle tensed; muscle ticked at the side; muscle twitched; nervous tics jerked along; opened; rested against; rested on; set; softened; squared; tensed; tightened; twitched.

Verbs – Things That Can Be Done to the Jaw

caressed; cracked; cut; elbowed; jabbed; kissed; kissed along; kissed the line of; licked; lips caressed beneath; lips slid to the curve of; lips traveled to; nudged; poked; prodded; punched; rubbed; rubbed at; scratched; scratched at it; shaved; slapped; slashed at; smoothed; smoothed over; sucked along; swung at; tapped; took in hand.

Descriptive Phrases

A muscle in his jaw ticked.

Dark stubble marked his hard angular jaw line.

He rubbed his jaw line thoughtfully.

His jaw tightened in anger.

The dark shadow of stubble roughened his jaw line.

11
Words and Phrases to Describe the Neck

Root Words

neck; neckline; spine.

Adjectives

ashen; bold; broad; brown; chiseled; cold; creamy; delicate; divine; elegant; exposed; feminine; graceful; hard; hot; icy; limp; marmoreal; masculine; muscular; pale; regal; relaxed; sculpted; sinewy; smooth; stiff; strong; swan-like; tanned; tense; thick; thin; warm.

Descriptive Combinations

base of her neck; by the scruff of the neck; curve of her neck; hollow at the base of her neck; nape of her neck; pain in the neck; smooth column of her neck; smooth skin on his neck; soft skin of her neck; strong column of his neck; tendons on her neck.

Verbs – Things the Neck Can Do

arched; bent; blushed; blush rose up; bulged; burned; contorted; cracked; craned; creaked; exposed; felt hand on; gave out; hardened; heat crept up; leaned to one side; leveled off; pink spots broke out on; pinpricks trickled down; pulse beat in; reared; relaxed; rested against; rested on; retreated;

seared; shot out; shot up; smoldered; spasmed; stiffened; strained; tensed; tension coiled in; turned; twisted; warmed; withdrew.

Verbs – Things That Can Be Done to the Neck

arms encircled; bit; breathed down; breath fanned against; breath whispered across; broke; buried head against; burrowed into; caressed; clasped hands together behind; clung to; curls swept up from; dropped kisses on; dug into; encircled; eyes moved down; eyes moved over; fingers brushed nape of; focused on; gaze traveled up over; grabbed the back of; hand curved around; hand lingered at back of; hands brushed; hooked arm around; hooked hand around; hummed into; hung around; kissed; knocked across back of; leaned on; licked; linked hands behind; manipulated; massaged; nuzzled; patted the back of; planted kiss on; poured over; pressed; pressed kisses on; pressed kiss to; raised face from; ran hand across back of; ran tip of tongue over; ran tongue over; rubbed; rubbed fingers across the back of; sank teeth into; scraped; scratched; skimmed kisses over; slapped; slid arms around; slid hand around; slipped fingers to side of; smothered; stroked; sucked; surveyed; tasted; tongue traced; touched; trailed kisses over; visited; whispered against; whispered into; wrapped arms around; wrung.

Descriptive Phrases

Her hand brushed over his head and settled on the back of his neck.

He trailed open-mouth kisses along the underside of her neck.

Pinpricks trickled down the length of her neck.

She could feel his warm breath on her neck.

The hairs on the back of her neck began to prickle.

12
Words and Phrases to Describe Shoulders

Adjectives

athletic; beefy; big; bony; brawny; broad; brown; bulky; burly; creamy; dark; delicate; dependable; expansive; feeble; feminine; god-like; hard; hearty; heavy; herculean; husky; imposing; invulnerable; light; marble-like; masculine; mighty; muscular; narrow; never-ending; pale; perfect; powerful; resolute; robust; rugged; satin; scrawny; silk-clad; sinewy; skinny; slight; slim; smooth; stalwart; stiff; stout; straight; strapping; strong; sturdy; supple; tanned; taut; thick; thin; toned; trim; unfaltering; unwavering; white; wide.

Descriptive Combinations

a weight fell off her shoulders; broad satin-smooth shoulders; head and shoulders above; pale smooth skin of her shoulders; smooth white shoulders; weight of the world on her shoulders; wide, strong shoulders.

Verbs – Things Shoulders Can Do

bared; barged; braced; drooped; faltered; flexed; held; hunched; lowered; moved; pressed against; pulled down; raised; relaxed; relaxed against; rippled; rolled; shook; shrank in; slumped; squared; steadied; stiffened; straightened; stretched back; stretched out; tensed; threw back; tightened; tipped back; wavered.

Verbs – Things That Can Be Done to Shoulders

accentuated; arm tightened around; bounced about; braced weight on; brushed; caressed; clung to; combed; curved an arm around; descended en masse to; draped across; dug fingers into; dug nails into; eased a jacket from; eyes touched on; fell past; fingers bit into; gripped; hair bounced on; hair cascaded over; hair rippled across; hair splayed across; hands settled down on; hands slid up to; hands smoothed over; hugged; kneaded; massaged; nestled against; palms skimmed across; passed around; pinched; planted hands on; pulled down; punched; pushed against; pushed it off; rested against; rested on; rubbed; sat upon; scraped against; scratched; scratched at; shook; shucked the dress from; slapped; smoothed; stared at; surrounded; took; trailed fingers across; tugged; wrapped hands around.

Descriptive Phrases

Her palms skimmed across his satin-smooth shoulders.

He turned around and pressed his shoulders up against the door.

She clung to his broad shoulders.

She grabbed onto his thick muscular shoulders and hoisted herself up onto his back.

She marveled at the breadth of his shoulders.

13
Words and Phrases to Describe the Chest

Adjectives

athletic; bare; broad; bronzed; defined; delicious; exposed; firm; gleaming; gorgeous; hair-roughened; hard; impeccable; masculine; mesmerizing; muscled; muscular; naked; powerful; pumped; raw; rock-hard; sculpted; solid; strong; tanned; taut; thick; tight; warm; well-built.

Descriptive Combinations

bare-chested; broad and powerful chest; broad expanse of chest; finely sculpted muscles of his chest; hair-roughened chest; hard ridges of his chest; hard warm chest; immaculately sculpted chest; muscular male chest; smoothly muscled chest; solid wall of male chest; warmth of his chest; well-developed muscles of his chest.

Verbs – Things the Chest Can Do (Internal & External)

abraded; ache blossomed in; ached; adrenaline spread through; anger tightened; beat; burned; compressed; constricted feeling in; distress crowded; dropped; expanded; exploded; fear flooded; fell; felt a response in; felt a slight easing in; felt like it had been hit; felt tight; filled; filled up; flooded; frustration built in; gleamed in the light; grew heavy; hardened; heart pounded in; heart pounding against; heaved; heavy numbness invaded; held close to; held to; hugged it tightly to; hurt; intense emotion filled; lifted; meshed with her breasts; opened; opened up; pain in; pain laced; pain seized; puffed out; pushed forward; rose; rubbed against;

rumbled against; satisfaction burning in; scraped; scraped against; seized tight; seized up tight; shook; slight twinge in; spread from; squeezed tight with pain; strained; strange twinge in; tightened; trembled; twisted.

Verbs – Things That Can Be Done to the Chest

beat; breasts brushed against; breasts met; breasts pressed against; breasts pushed against; caressed; clutched against; clutched tightly to; connected with; contacted with; covered; curled up against; eyes met; fell against; fingers flexed against; folded arms across; folded arms over; growled low in; hand drifted over; heart beat hard against; hit; hugged; knees drawn up to; lay against; leaned on; legs drawn up to; lowered (her) mouth to; made contact with; moved hands over; nipples pressed into; placed palms flat over; pointed to; pressed on; pushed at; put arms around; put hands on; put hand to; ran hands down; rested on; roved over; rubbed; rubbed against; rubbed face back and forth across; sank into; scraped; scraped down; settled against; skimmed across; skimmed over; slid against; slid mouth over; smacked; smacked across; snuggled against; snuggled to; stroked; thumped; tickled.

Descriptive Phrases

He felt a hole in his chest where his heart should be.

His chest was a work of art.

His heart swelled in his chest.

His hard chest felt delicious against her breasts.

She pressed her hands hard against his chest.

14
Words and Phrases to Describe Breasts

Root Words

apexes; apices; boobs; bosoms; bounty; breasts; bust; chest; cleavage; curves; flesh; fruits; glands; globes; mounds; orbs; ovals; pair; peaks; swells; tits; towers.

Adjectives

aching; ample; aroused; bare; bared; beautiful; beautifully-formed; big; bountiful; brazen; burgeoning; burning; bursting; chubby; creamy; curved; curvy; delicious; eager; engorged; exposed; feminine; firm; fleshy; flushed; free; fresh; full; glistening; hard; hardening; heaving; heavy; honey-soft; hot; jiggling; juicy; jutting; large; luscious; lush; magnificent; milky; mouth-watering; naked; natural; not large; pale; pendant; perfect; perky; pert; pink-tipped; plump; pouting; ripe; rosy; round; rounded; sensitive; shimmering; silky; sizable; small; smooth; soft; squeezable; still-blossoming; succulent; suckable; sweet; swollen; tasty; taut; tender; throbbing; thrusting; trembling; voluptuous; warm; well-formed.

Descriptive Combinations

aching, hardening flesh; ample cleavage; aroused peaks; beautifully-formed breasts; burgeoning apices; burgeoning swell; creamy flesh; delicious feminine curves; engorged boobs; fleshy pair; forbidden fruits;

full, round breasts; heaving bosom; ivory towers; luscious peaks; pert mounds; pink-tipped peaks; plump mounds; ripe flesh; silken swell; soft, ripe bounty; surging peaks; sweetly curved mounds; swelling flesh; swollen bounty; the swells of her desire; trembling apices; twin towers; warm tingling flesh.

Verbs – Things Breasts Can Do

ached; bared; bounced; burst free; dangled; exposed; fell; grazed; heaved; jiggled; pressed against; rose; skimmed; slapped against; spilled forward; spilled out; splashed against; swayed; swelled; taunted; teased; throbbed; thrust forward; tightened; tingled; warmed.

Verbs – Things That Can Be Done to Breasts

bit; captured; caressed; caught one; charted; circled; clasped; clinched; crushed; cuddled; cupped; embraced; fondled; found; freed; hugged; kissed; kneaded; lapped; licked; massaged; milked; molded; nibbled; nipped; palmed; plumped; pressed; reshaped; rubbed; scooped; showcased; slapped; slurped; squeezed; stroked; sucked; suckled; tasted; tested the weight of.

Descriptive Phrases

He caressed her throbbing bosoms, molding and reshaping them with satisfaction.

He cupped her swollen breasts.

He stared down at her ample cleavage, marveling at the sheer size of her bounty.

He unfastened her bra, grunting as her breasts spilled excitedly against his chest.

She smoothed over her breasts with palm oil.

15
Words and Phrases to Describe Nipples

Root Words

apex; areola; bud; bulge; bump; center; crest; diamond; kernel; lump; nib; nipple; nub; nubbin; nubble; peak; pebble; point; prominence; protrusion; protuberance; tip.

Adjectives

aroused; bare; beading; burning; delectable; dimpled; distended; dusky; erect; flushed; hard; hardened; hardening; inflamed; lactating; large; little; marble-hard; peaked; pearled; pebble-hard; perky; pert; petite; pink; plump; pointed; pointy; pokey; prickly; protruding; protuberant; pulsing; quivering; raw; rigid; rising; rose-colored; rose-red; rose-tipped; rosy; salty; sensitive; small; stiff; stinging; swollen; tanned; tantalizing; taut; tender; throbbing; tight; tingling; turgid; velvet; waiting; weeping; wet.

Descriptive Combinations

aching peak; bare tip; crested peak; dark pink areola; dusky crest; dusky tip; engorged tip; flushed red areola; hardened peak; hard little dagger-point; hard point; heated bud; little pebble; melon-colored centers; most delicate point; pale pink buds; peaked, rosebud nipple; peaked rosebud of desire; peaked tip; pearled tip; pebbled pink nub; pebbled tip; proud nubbin; proud peak; quivering tip; rigid rose-red peak; ring of color; ripe bud; rock-like point; rose colored areola; rosy crest; rosy diamond;

sensitive peak; shimmering bud; silken tip; stiff crest; taut pebble; tender crest; throbbing peak; throbbing tip; thrusting point; tight bud; tightly beaded nub; tiny pink bud; tiny rigid nub; velvet peak.

Verbs – Things Nipples Can Do

ached; beaded; became sensitive; brushed across; brushed against; contracted; expanded; gleamed; grew large; grew rigid; hardened; oozed; peaked; pouted; puckered; pulsed; pushed against; rose; shivered erect; sprang to attention; stood at attention; stood up; swelled; tautened; throbbed; tightened; tingled; weeped/wept.

Verbs – Things That Can Be Done to Nipples

blew across; brushed; captured; captured between his lips/fingers; caressed; chafed his thumb over; circled; clamped; closed around; drew into his mouth; encircled; fingered; flicked; found; grabbed; grasped; kissed; kneaded; lapped; lashed; latched onto; licked; nibbled; nipped; pinched; pinned between his fingers/teeth; played with; probed; ringed; rolled; rolled between his fingers/teeth; rubbed; shaped; smothered; sucked; suckled; swiped; tasted; teased; took it between his teeth; touched; tugged; tweaked; twisted; wet; whisked; worked.

Descriptive Phrases

He lashed the tip of her nipple with his tongue.

Her nipples felt like little pebbles against his chest.

Her nipples were as hard as sharp dagger points.

He teased the tight rosy bud of her nipple between his fingers.

He took her dark pink areola into his mouth, sucking vigorously.

16
Words and Phrases to Describe the Heart

Adjectives

big; bitter; black; blackened; broken; broken-hearted; cold; cold-hearted; cool; dead; delicate; enormous; evil; galloping; good; granite-hearted; hard; heart-stopping; heartache; heartless; heavy; kind; kind-hearted; light; light-hearted; little; pained; prideful; romantic; steady; sweetheart; tender; tender-hearted; trapped; treacherous; unfettered; vulnerable; warm; warm-hearted; wicked.

Descriptive Combinations

change of heart; hand to her heart; heart-beat raged out of control; heart in her throat; heart in the right place; heart of a lion; heart was in her mouth; her heart on her sleeve; her heart skipped a beat; hole where her heart used to be; loved with all her heart; nursing a broken heart; pinch in her chest; pulse of his heart; romantic little heart; room in her heart; set her heart on; steady beat of his heart; tempo of his heart; thumped like a piston; thunderous beat of her heart; thunderous thumping of his heart; wished with all her heart; with a heavy heart.

Verbs – Things the Heart Can Do

ached; battered her breastbone; beat hard against chest; beat like a drum; blossomed; boiled; bounced; burned; burned for; caught; clunked against ribs; constricted; contorted; contracted; curled up; danced; demanded; dived; dropped into stomach; expanded; fell; felt an electric jolt; felt in;

felt it stop in chest; fluttered; galloped; gave out; grew; hammered against chest; hammered behind breastbone; hammered below breastbone; hammered in chest; hammered out of chest; heart-beat kicked up speed; heart-rate quickened; heart-rate rocketed; heart-rate sped up; hurt; jumped; leaped; leaped in chest; leapt; lifted; loved; lurched; missed a beat; murmured; needed; overflowed with emotion; pained; pinched; plummeted; pounded; pulsated; raced; raged in chest; rattled; rebelled; recoiled; resisted; responded; rested; rose up; sang; sank; seethed; seized up; settled; shriveled up; skipped; skipped a beat; squeezed; stalled; started beating faster; steadied; stopped; stumbled; stuttered; swelled; swelled with love; swooned; thudded; thumped against ribs; thundered in chest; ticked; tightened; told; tripped; tripped over itself; tripped up; tumbled in chest; turned over on itself; twirled; twisted; wanted; worked up; wrenched; wrenched up tight.

Verbs – Things That Can Be Done to the Heart

attacked; begged for; broke; caught; chipped away at; clutched at; demanded; destroyed; eat at; felt the beat of; found; grief filled; heard; hurt; listened to; loved; needed; offered; offered up; pierced; seized; shared; sliced through; stabbed; stole; strangled; struck; suffocated; threatened; torn from chest; touched; trampled beneath feet; trampled on; tugged at; waited for; wanted; warmed; would kill for.

Descriptive Phrases

A dark, sickening grief filled her heart.

He could feel the thunderous beat of her heart.

Her heart began beating like a drum in her chest.

Her heart pounded so loudly in her ears that thought she might go deaf.

Her heart stumbled before finding its rhythm once again.

Her heart ticked like an over-wound clock.

His heart responded, thumping hard and steady against his chest.

17
Words and Phrases to Describe Arms

Parts of the Arm

wrist; forearm; elbow; crook of the arm; bicep; tricep; upper-arm

Adjectives

accepting; bare; beefy; boney; bronzed; bulging; chiseled; corded; defined; flexed; hard; lean; meaty; muscular; protective; pulsing; pumped; secure; shapely; short; silky smooth; sinewy; skinny; slender; smooth; soft; solid; stocky; straining; strong; tanned; tattooed; taut; thick; thin; tiny; toned; tough; veiny; well-built.

Descriptive Combinations

chiseled triceps; hard, pumped arms; long, slender arms; muscular forearms; pale thin arms; sinewy biceps; smooth, skinny arms; strong protective arms.

Verbs – Things Arms Can Do

came around; carried in; circled; claimed; clamped around; closed around; coiled around; collected; contorted; covered; cradled around; cradled in; crossed; crushed; curled around; curved around; draped across; draped over the edge; draped through; drew back; dropped; encircled; extended; flexed;

flung around; folded; folded across; gathered into; grabbed in; guarded; held; held in; jerked; knotted around; lifted; linked; locked around; looped around; looped through; offered; opened; opened; parted; picked up in; pinned; pressed against; protected; pulled away; pulled into; pushed up with; put around; put at; relaxed; rested; rested on top of; rocked back and forth; scooped up into; shaded; sheltered; shielded; shifted; shivered; shook; slid around; slid behind; slid into; spread; spread open; stretched around; stretched forward; supported; surrounded; swept into; swept up in; swung around; taken into; threw around; thrown over; tightened around; took in; torqued around; tucked beneath; twisted around; warmed; wiped with; wound around; wrapped around.

Verbs – Things That Can Be Done to Arms

accepted; brushed hand over; caught; clung to; collapsed into; dragged; entered; escaped; flew into; forced; found; found in; grabbed; grabbed onto; grasped; gripped; hand fastened around; hung from; hung on; jerked out of; jumped into; kissed; leaped into; licked; lifted; lost composure in; loved; melted in; moved on; pinched; pinned; placed in; pressed against; pushed away; put hand on; ran from; relaxed in; rested against; slapped; slept in; slid hand down; slid hand over; slid out beneath; snuggled in; squeezed; stroked; tears splashed onto; took; took hold of; touched; tugged; twisted; wriggled free from.

Descriptive Phrases

He pulled her into his arms.

He swept her up in his arms.

She crossed her arms beneath her breasts.

She smoothed over his strong protective arms.

She wrapped her arms around his neck.

18
Words and Phrases to Describe Hands

Root Words

hand; palm.

Adjectives

big; brown; calloused; chubby; cold; comforting; damp; delicate; dirty; drowsy; dry; feminine; fine-boned; fluid; gentle; heavy; hot; icy; impatient; large; lean; little; masculine; pale; petite; podgy; powerful; rough; scarred; slender; small; smooth; soft; strong; supple; trembling; warm; wet.

Descriptive Combinations

big powerful hands; chubby little hand; heel of a hand; large, masculine hand; palm of his hand; rough and sweaty hand; smooth, supple hands; soft, pale hands; strong, warm hands; sun-kissed hands.

Verbs – Things a Hand Can Do

balled up; braced on; bracketed; brought up; brushed; brushed against; brushed over; bunched up; came up; captured; clenched; clenched into fists; closed; closed around; clutched; covered; crossed over; cupped; curled around; curled into fists; curved; dismissed; drew over; dropped; dug into; eased around; eased below; enveloped; extended; fell; flew up;

glided; gripped; handed; hovered; knotted into fists; lifted; locked; lowered; moved; moved between; moved through; offered; opened; picked up; planted on; poured over; pressed against; pulled; pulled back; pushed; put on; put over; raised; ran down; ran over; ran through; reached out; removed; rested on; roamed over; rushed over; rushed toward; sank into; shifted; shook; shot out; showed; slammed down; slid down; slipped beneath; splayed; spread; stretched down; stretched out; swept up; swept up over; threw; threw up; tightened into fists; touched; trembled; tucked below; tugged; waved; wrapped around.

Verbs – Things That Can Be Done to a Hand

accepted; captured; covered; freed; grabbed; grasped; gripped; held; held up; looked at; looked down at; patted; picked up; reached for; rubbed; slapped; slapped away; tickled; took; touched; tugged; turned.

Descriptive Phrases

He captured her hands in his.

He clenched his hands into fists and pounded on the door.

He took her hand in his.

She had him eating out of the palm of her hand.

The gentle and fluid motion of her hand on his face gain birth to a swarm of butterflies in his stomach.

19
Words and Phrases to Describe Fingers

Root Words

finger; fingernail; fingertip; forefinger; thumb.

Adjectives

agitated; angry; blunt; brown; careless; cold; daring; deft; delicate; desperate; engagement; feminine; fiery; gentle; helpful; highly effective; hot; impatient; knowing; lean; light; little; long; male; manicured; masculine; middle; nervous; nimble; playful; possessive; powerful; reproving; restive; ring; rough; shaking; silencing; silken; skilled; skillful; slender; slim; starfish; stiff; strong; sure; taunting; teasing; tentative; trembling; warm; wedding; wedding-ring; white; wondering.

Descriptive Combinations

blunt masculine fingers; imperious set of long fingers; long brown fingers; long fingers; naked wedding-ring finger; nervously clenching fingers; set of fingers; strong male fingers.

Verbs – Things Fingers Can Do

anchored to; bit into; brushed; brushed across; came into contact with; caressed; caught between; clenched; clenched together; closed around;

combed; crossed; cupped; curled; dallied; danced over; delved into; dipped in; drew along; drove through; drummed; dug into; enclosed; entwined into; fanned out across; feathered over; fingered; flexed; flexed over; flicked; flipped; fluffed; forked through; found; framed; glided along; glided up; grabbed; grasped; gripped; held between; hooked in; hovered over; knotted; laced into; laced together; laid on; lifted; lodged in; massaged between; pointed; probed; pushed into; raked over; raked through; ran across; ran below; ran down between; reached; released; rested against; rested below; roamed; rolled between; rose; sank (deep) inside; sank into; skated over; skimmed; slid inside; slid up; smoothed back; smoothed over; snapped; sought; splayed across; spread; squeezed; straightened; stroked; stroked over; stumbled; sucked into; tangled in; teased; threaded; threaded through; thrust; tightened; tightened around; tilted up; tingled; tipped up; took between; tormented; touched; tousled; toyed with; traced; trailed; trailed through; trailed up over; tugged; tugged free; wound around; wound into; wrapped around.

Verbs – Things That Can Be Done to Fingers

adorned; carried down; drained through; eased onto; enveloped; grabbed; grasped; licked; lifted; looked down at; massaged on; placed on; put on; released; slid onto; squeezed; sucked; suckled; tasted.

Descriptive Phrases

He glided his deft fingers down her back and planted his hand firmly on her behind.

He ran his fingers over her smooth skin.

Her fingers threaded through his hair.

Her long fingers dug into the taut flesh of his back.

His fingers danced over her flat stomach before finding her silky smooth thigh.

His nimble fingers teased her nipple, making it grow rock-hard.

She drew a line along his chiseled jaw with her index finger.

20
Words and Phrases to Describe the Back

Adjectives

aquiline; bare; beautiful; bronzed; bulging; chiseled; contoured; curving; divine; elegant; flushed; god-like; hard; hunched; lean; marble-hard; mountainous; muscular; narrow; pale; perfect; posture-perfect; ramrod-straight; rippling; sculpted; sensuous; slender; slim; soft; straight; sublime; supple; tanned; taut; trim; warm; well-balanced; well-defined; wide.

Descriptive Combinations

contour of her back; curving lines of her back; get off my back; pain in the back; posture-perfect back; rippling muscles of his back; strong, powerful back; taut muscles of his back.

Verbs – Things the Back Can Do

ached; arched; bent; bowed; came against; coiled; cracked; curved; fell; fell back; fell on; flushed; grazed; hunched; jerked; laid down on; landed on; leaned; leaned back; loosened; lurched; narrowed; perspired; pivoted; relaxed; rolled over on; rounded; sat back; shivered; shook; slumped; spasmed; straightened; stretched; supported; tensed; tightened; tingled; twisted; widened.

Verbs – Things That Can Be Done to the Back

bit; broke; clawed at; dug nails into; gnawed; gripped; heated; held; hit; hooked; kicked; kissed; kneaded; licked; massaged; nibbled on; nipped; petted; pinched; pressed; pressed down on; punched; ran hand up and down; rubbed; scraped; scratched; slapped; slid palms down; smacked; smoothed over; smothered; stroked; warmed; wet.

Descriptive Phrases

He landed flat on his back, the air escaping his lungs.

He reveled in the beautiful curving lines of her sensuous back.

Her fingertips traced the bulging muscles in his back.

She arched her back as waves of ecstasy pulsed through her body.

She gently gnawed on his upper back, hoping the warmth she felt would never end.

21
Words and Phrases to Describe the Bottom

Root Words

arse; ass; backside; behind; bottom; bum; buns; butt; buttocks; derrière; gluteus maximus; haunches; mounds; posterior; rear; rear end; rump; tush.

Adjectives

adorable; attractive; beautiful; chubby; delectable; flat; fleshy; hot; large; lean; lissom; little; lovely; lumpy; luxurious; milky; mouth-watering; muscular; pale; perfect; petite; plump; round; sexy; silky; slim; small; smooth; soft; supple; swollen; tanned; taut; tender; toned; warm; well-rounded.

Descriptive Combinations

adorable, little ass; busted their butts; cheeks of his derrière; lovely swollen cheeks; perfect, toned bottom; two lovely mounds.

Verbs – Things the Bottom Can Do

clenched; flexed; glistened; hugged; moved; opened; parted; perspired; positioned; relaxed; rested on; sat; settled; shifted; shook; stuck out; tensed; thrust out; tightened; tingled; trembled; turned.

Verbs – Things That Can Be Done to the Bottom

bit; brushed; caressed; caught; cupped; encircled; explored; exposed; eyes strayed to; eyes took in; fingers danced over; fingers moved over; glanced at; gripped; hand landed on; held; held; kissed; licked; lifted; looked at; massaged; moved over; noticed; petted; pinched; placed hand on; pounded; raised; ran hands over; rubbed; showed off; skimmed over; slapped; slid down; slid palms over; smacked; smoothed over; snared; spanked; squeezed; stared at; sucked; supported; swept over; tightened hold on; took; touched; weighed.

Descriptive Phrases

He slid his warm and powerful hands over her smooth bum.

He trailed his fingertips down her back and found her soft buttocks.

She bent over the chair and showed off her delectable derrière.

She stole a quick glance at his toned bottom.

With a fiery determination he scooped her up, squeezing hard her behind.

22
Words and Phrases to Describe the Abdomen and Stomach

Root Words

abdomen; abdominal muscles; abs; love handles; lower abdomen; middle; midriff; midsection; stomach.

Adjectives

accentuated; bare; bronzed; brown; bulging; chiseled; cold; creamy; dark; defined; fevered; flabby; flat; flip-flopping; hair-roughened; hard; hot; icy; muscular; pale; quivering; raw; remarkable; ripped; sculpted; slim; smooth; supple; swollen; tanned; taut; tense; tight; toned; trim; velvet; warm; washboard; well-defined; white.

Descriptive Combinations

a heavy weight settled in her stomach; don't have the stomach for it; flat as a washboard; pit of her stomach; tense muscles of his stomach.

Verbs – Things the Abdomen and Stomach Can Do

bubbled; burned with emotion; churned; clenched; contracted; cramped;

curdled; curled; dove; dropped; fell; felt butterflies in; felt ill; felt nauseous; felt nerves dance in; felt sensitive; felt sick; fluttered; free-fell groaned; growled; gyrated; hurt; knotted; laid on; lifted; lurched; nausea bubbled in; nausea stirred in; pained; plunged; quivered; rumbled; sank; settled; sick feeling curdled in; spun; stirred; swirled; tensed; throbbed; tightened; tugged at; twisted; twisted inside.

Verbs – Things That Can Be Done to the Abdomen and Stomach

brushed over; caressed; charted; cuddled; embraced; explored; exposed; eyes strayed to; fingers danced over; fingers moved over; fingers slid down over; found; hand landed on; hand moved up and down; hand slid down; hand swept over; hit; hugged; kissed; lapped; leaned against; licked; nipped; palmed; placed hand on; pressed; pressed against; pressed against; punched in; ran hand over; rubbed; settled on; skimmed across; skimmed over; slid forward onto; smoothed over; stabbed at; stroked; tasted; touched.

Descriptive Phrases

Her stomach contracted and a rush of heat flooded her entire body.

Her stomach rumbled and she realized she'd missed lunch.

His stomach felt as though it had been anchored with a heavy weight.

His strong powerful hand gently pressed against her stomach.

The mere presence of him caused her stomach to clench tight.

23
Words and Phrases to Describe the Hips and Waist

Root Words

hipbone; hips; middle; pelvis; waist.

Adjectives

aesthetic; ample; appealing; attractive; balanced; bare; child-baring; comely; creamy; curvaceous; curvesome; curvy; desirable; dramatic; enthusiastic; enticing; erotic; exquisite; fleshly; full-figured; hourglass; large; lean; limber; lithe; luscious; lush; narrow; petite; pleasure-seeking; provocative; refined; round; rounded; sensual; sensuous; sexy; shapely; sleek; slender; slight; small; smooth; statuesque; streamlined; stunning; sweeping; tenuous; thin; tiny; trim; voluptuous; wanton; well-rounded; wide.

Descriptive Combinations

bare skin of her waist; flare of her hip; hands on hips; indent of her waist; rhythm of his hips; round, shapely hips; rounded curve of her hip; smooth white skin of her hip; sway of her hips.

Verbs – Things the Hips and Waist Can Do

ached; arched; balked; bucked; bucked forward; cocked to the side;

contorted; convulsed; dipped; dithered; drew back; dug into; faltered; gave way; gyrated; jerked; jolted; kicked; leaned; lifted; lowered; moved; nudged with; pinned; pressed against; pulsated; pumped up and down; quaked; raised; reeled; relaxed; rocked back and forth; shifted; shimmied; shivered; shook; shuddered; spasmed; steadied; stilled; swayed; swung; tensed; thrust upward; tightened; tingled; trembled; vibrated; wavered; wobbled.

Verbs – Things That Can Be Done to the Hips and Waist

anchored hands around; arms came around; arms tightened around; bounced up and down on; came around; circled; claimed; clamped around; closed around; coiled around; cupped; curled around; encircled; erection pressed hard against; exposed; fingers curled against; gripped; ground into; hands spanned; hands splayed on; held; hugged; kissed; knotted around; leg hooked over; legs bounced about on either side of; legs curled around; legs hugged; legs snug against; legs tight against; locked around; locked legs around; looped around; planted hands on; propped on; pulled down onto; pushed dress up past; pushed jeans down; put hand on; put hands on either side of; rested hands on; rested on top of; settled in the cradle of; slid down; slipped arm around; stretched around; tied low on; tightened around; twisted around; wound around; wrapped around; wrapped legs around.

Descriptive Phrases

Her hips thrust in a steady rhythm, edging her closer to the breaking point.

He slipped an arm around her narrow waist.

He trailed hot open-mouth kisses across the length of her slim waistline.

She undid her zipper and let the dress slide down her hips and onto the floor.

Without thinking, he grabbed her by the waist and crushed her body to his.

24
Words and Phrases to Describe the Penis

Root Words

arousal; bulge; brand; cock; core; dick; eagerness; erection; extension; flesh; fullness; girth; groin; hardness; heat; hotness; instrument; length; length of him; loins; maleness; manhood; masculinity; member; organ; part of him; penis; phallus; rigidity; rod; sex; shaft; staff; stalk; tumescence; virility.

Genital-Related Words

pubic bone; nest; plumage
head; tip; glans
foreskin
shaft; length
urethra; opening; hole
base
balls; testicle; testes
scrotum; sac
cum; semen; precum; fluid; liquid; cream; nectar

Adjectives

aching; aggressive; aroused; beautiful; blatant; bloated; bold; brimming; bruised; brutal; bulbous; bulging; burgeoning; coarse; creamy; distended; eager; engorged; enlarged; enormous; erect; expanding; fiery; firm; fleshy; full; growing; hard; hardened; hot; iron-hard; juicy; jutting; lengthening;

long; lustful; magnificent; mammoth; masculine; massive; molten; painful; panty-scorching; pounding; powerful; proud; pulsating; pulsing; quivering; raging; rigid; rock-hard; scorching; silky; sinewy; smelting; smoldering; solid; spongy; staunch; steamy; steely; stiff; stirring; straining; striking; strong; surging; sweet; swelling; swollen; thick; thickening; throbbing; torrid; tumescent; tumid; turgid; veiny; velvety; virile; wooden.

Descriptive Combinations

aching arousal; aching bulge; aching erection; aggressive, pulsating cock; aroused flesh; aroused organ; below the belt; bulging erection; burgeoning erection; distended flesh; eager maleness; engorged flesh; engorged shaft; erect manhood; fiery brand; firm flesh; full, throbbing erection; growing arousal; growing erection; hardened shaft; hard male heat; his source of heat; his source of masculinity; hot flesh; hungry bulge; iron-hard tumescence; lower half; lustful loins; magnificent arousal; male member; mammoth cock; massive dick; molten member; painful girth; powerful masculinity; pulsing core; quivering member; raging erection; rigid flesh; rigid part of him; rigid shaft; silky member; sinewy staff; smoldering rod; steely length; stirring manhood; straining erection; straining masculinity; swollen flesh; that part of him that made him male; the evidence of his arousal; the hardness of his arousal; the hard pulse of his arousal; the swelling in his loins; the sword of his desire; thrusting hardness; torrid extension; tortured flesh; tumescent core; turgid organ; turgid shaft; virile masculinity; virile member.

Verbs – Things a Penis Can Do

battered; blossomed; dangled; dribbled; dripped; eased in; ejaculated; ejected; entered; expanded; filled her up; grew; gushed; hammered; impaled; inserted; jabbed; jutted against her; nudged; oozed; penetrated; ploughed; pounded; probed; pulsated; pulsed; pummeled; pumped; punched; sank into her; slapped against; slid; slipped; spilled; sprang forth; sprayed; squirted; stimulated; thickened; throbbed; thrust; withdrew.

Verbs – Things That Can Be Done to a Penis

beat; bit; blew; blew on; caressed; coddled; cradled; encircled; engulfed; enveloped; gripped; hand-stroked; jerked off; kneaded; lathered up; licked;

massaged; milked; rubbed; slobbered over; spat on; squeezed; stroked; sucked; teased; took hold of.

Descriptive Phrases

Her fingertips skated across the aching bulge in his pants.

Her hands tightened even more around his straining shaft.

Her lips tightly encircled his throbbing manhood.

Her slight, elegant figure brought a hardness to his loins.

His cock had blossomed into a thick, swollen masterpiece.

She aggressively grabbed his manhood with both hands, feeling the hardness rise in him.

She continued the slow and steady motion, sliding up and down his engorged flesh.

She massaged the hot, smooth column of flesh between her fingers then leaned down and began licking the swollen head.

With rapid circular motions, she explored the entire length of his shaft with her tongue.

25
Words and Phrases to Describe the Vulva and Vagina

Root Words

center; channel; cleft; core; cunt; depths; entrance; excitement; femininity; flaps; flesh; flower; folds; furnace; haven; heat; hole; junction; labia; lips; loins; moistness; mound; opening; orifice; pads; passage; pinkness; portal; pussy; sex; sheath; slit; softness; sweetness; tightness; vestibule; vulva; warmth; wetness; womanhood.

Genital-Related Words

pubic bone; nest; bush; plumage
outer labia; outer lips
inner labia; inner lips
clitoris; clit; nub; bud
urethra
hymen
vagina
g-spot
perineum
fluid; liquid; cream; nectar

Adjectives

bare; beautiful; damp; dank; delicate; downy; drenched; dripping; drizzling; enticing; fleshy; flowery; fragrant; glistening; golden; hot; juicy; little; lubricated; luscious; meaty; moist; molten; open; petite; plump; pulsating; ripe; satin; saturated; silk; silken; silky; slick; slippery; smoldering; smooth; soaked; soaking; sodden; soft; soggy; sopping; soppy; sparkling; sticky; succulent; swollen; tender; tight; vaginal; virginal; warm; wet; womanly.

Descriptive Combinations

apex of her legs; bare flesh; between her creamy hips; between her legs; between her thighs; center of paradise; cleft between her legs; core of her being; curls between her legs; curls of her center; curly mound of tawny hair; damp, moist needy place; dampness between her legs; damp petals of her womanhood; deeper heat within; deep recesses of her; delicate softness; door of her femininity; downy mound; entrance of her femininity; fiery furnace; golden flesh; guarded place; hot, wet sheath; hot pool; inner thighs; interior muscles; into her body; juncture of her thighs; liquid heat between her thighs; moist center; moist heart of her; moistness between her legs; moist sex; moist warm folds between her thighs; molten need; most secret place; most sensitive spot; most special of places; most tender flesh; most treasured pearl of passion; nest of curls at the junction of her thighs; nest of hair between her thighs; nest of moist curls; nether lips; passion-moistened depths; petal-smooth center; petal-soft folds of her womanhood; place even warmer and wetter; portals of her womanhood; private satin flesh; pulsating core; receptive body; secret center; secret parts; slick folds; slick wet heat of her; slick wetness of her excitement; slippery softness; slit between her legs; soft flesh; stretching walls of her body; sweet warmth; throbbing core; tight, wet womanhood; tight depths; tight passage; warm, dark haven; warm damp entrance; warm slit; warmth between her legs; where she most ached for fulfillment; where she was moist and desperate; womanly center of her; womanly folds; womanly heart of her; womanly secrets.

Verbs – Things Female Genitals Can Do

clamped; constricted; diffused; discharged; drizzled; fastened around; locked around; locked onto; spilled; spread; spread wide; squeezed;

squelched; tightened; tightened around; throbbed; tingled; trembled; widened.

Verbs – Things That Can Be Done to Female Genitals

chewed; demolished; devastated; dipped into; drove into; filled; forced apart; ground; kissed; kneaded; lapped; licked; massaged; nibbled; nudged; penetrated; pillaged; plundered; plunged into; pounded; pulverized; pumped; pushed into; rubbed; sank into; skimmed over; slapped; slipped into; slurped; spat on; spread it open; sucked; tapped; thrust into.

Descriptive Phrases

He kissed the moist warm folds between her thighs.

Her pink womanly center pulsated and tingled with pleasure.

He thrust his hips and sank into the cleft between her legs.

His fingers delved into her delicate softness making her buck forward.

His long fingers swept over her most guarded place.

The thought of his girth inside her almost sent her over the edge.

26
Words and Phrases to Describe Thighs

Root Words

inner thigh; lower thigh; mid-thigh; outer thigh; thigh; upper thigh.

Adjectives

bare; big; brown; craving; dainty; dark; delectable; delicate; delicious; elegant; glistening; hair-roughened; huge; large; lean; lissom; milky; moist; muscular; pale; perfect; petite; powerful; sinewy; slender; slim; soft; strong; supple; tanned; taut; tense; thick; thrusting; toned; warm.

Descriptive Combinations

apex of her thighs; hard shafts of his thighs; muscular shaft of his thighs; powerful thrust of his thighs; solidly carved thighs; strong brown thigh; taut and muscular thigh; thigh against thigh.

Verbs – Things Thighs Can Do

became hyper-sensitive; became numb; braced; brushed; burned; clenched; danced over; drew up; entwined around back; flexed; froze; glistened; got goosebumps; gripped; latched onto; leaned against; leaned on; levered between; moved; opened; parted; perspired; positioned; prickled; propped against; propped up; pushed between legs; relaxed muscles in; rested on;

shifted; shifted one onto the other; shivered; shook; spasmed; splayed against; spread; spread wide; squeezed; squeezed together; supported weight of; tensed; thrust; tightened; tightened around; tingled; trembled; wrapped around.

Verbs – Things That Can Be Done to Thighs

attention riveted on; brushed; caressed; dress clung to; drummed fingers against; encircled; exposed; eyes strayed to; eyes took in; fingers danced over; fingers moved over; gripped; hand landed on; hand moved down; hand moved over; hand moved up; hands braced against; hand slid down to; held; hem rode high on; hypnotized by; imagined; imagined parting; jeans stretched over; kissed; licked; looked at; mesmerized by; mouth smothered; noticed; opened; pinched; placed hand on; revealed; rubbed; settled between; slapped against; smacked against; stroked; swept hand down; tapped; teased; took; touched; tried not to notice; twined through; wrapped around.

Descriptive Phrases

Her thighs parted to receive his thrusting heat.

His attention was riveted on the pair of slender thighs that danced in front of the window.

His fingers began stroking feather-light touches over her glistening inner thigh.

His hand moved down to the soft skin of her inner thigh.

She held her breath as his fingertips teased the soft skin of her inner thigh.

27
Words and Phrases to Describe Legs

Root Words

calf; leg; upper leg.

Adjectives

bare; brown; chubby; dark; hair-roughened; jelly-like; lean; lissom; long; lovely; luxurious; milky; muscular; pale; perfect; petite; powerful; pudgy; rubbery; silken; silky; sinewy; slender; slim; smooth; soft; steady; stocking-clad; strong; supple; tanned; taut; thick; toned; warm; weak; wobbly.

Descriptive Combinations

cross-legged; her legs felt like jelly; long, lovely legs; long, stocking-clad legs; long, toned legs; muscular hair-roughened legs; smooth, lean legs; strong, tanned legs; thick, toned legs.

Verbs – Things Legs Can Do

braced; brushed; burned; clenched; crossed; crossed one over the other; curled around hips; drew up; entwined; fell open; flexed; froze; glistened; gripped; hooked around hips; hugged hips; laid; latched onto; lifted; moved; opened; parted; perspired; positioned; prickled; propped up; raised;

ran; recrossed; relaxed; rested on; sagged; settled; shifted; shivered; shook; showed off; skidded; skipped; slung over; spasmed; spread; spread open; steadied; stood up; stretched out; supported; tensed; thrust out; tightened; tightened around; tingled; trembled; turned; walked; weakened; wobbled; wrapped around.

Verbs – Things That Can Be Done to Legs

brushed; caressed; encased; encircled; exposed; eyes strayed to; eyes took in; fingers danced over; fingers moved over; forced apart; glanced at; gripped; hand landed on; hand moved over; hand moved up and down; hand slid down; hand swept over; held; hypnotized by; kissed; licked; lifted; looked at; mesmerized by; noticed; opened; parted; pinched; placed hand on; raised; ran hands over; revealed; riveted by; rubbed; settled on; shaved; skimmed hands over; slapped; slid arm under; slid down; slid hands up; smacked; stared at; stroked; sucked; tightened hold on; took; touched; tried not to notice.

Descriptive Phrases

Her legs weakened at his touch, and she melted helplessly into his warm body.

His hands skimmed gently over her wide hips and down her luxuriously silky legs.

His legs appeared long and powerful.

Sheer black stockings encased her lovely legs.

She wore a black miniskirt that showed off her long, toned legs.

28
Words and Phrases to Describe Feet

Adjectives

arched; bare; beautiful; big; bronzed; brown; cautious; clumsy; cold; creamy; curved; dancing; elegant; flat; graceful; hair-roughened; large; long; lovely; pale; petite; rough; sensitive; short; small; smooth; supple; tanned; tender; unwary; warm; wary; well-balanced; well-formed; white.

Descriptive Combinations

beautiful arching foot; beautiful, bronzed foot; followed in his footsteps; lost her footing; small, delicate feet; smooth, supple feet; stood barefoot; stood on her own two feet.

Verbs – Things Feet Can Do

balanced; bent; bounced; burrowed; contracted; crept; curled up; danced; dodged; dragged; got cold; hit; hobbled; hopped; hung; hustled; jogged; jumped; kicked; leaped; limped; marched; meandered; moved; nudged; plodded; poked; pounced; pranced; prodded; raced; ran; revolved; rocked; rolled; rotated; sauntered; scrambled; scuffed; scurried; shifted; shoved; shuffled; skipped; slapped; slipped; sprinted; sprung; spun; staggered; stalked; stamped; stood; stopped; strode; strolled; strutted; stumbled; tapped; tensed; tip-toed; tottered; trampled; tripped; trudged; turned; twirled; walked; zigzagged.

Verbs – Things That Can Be Done to Feet

caught; crept over to; explored; fitted with; forced into shoe; gripped; heard; kissed; kneaded; let towel drop to; licked; massaged; nibbled; nudged; petted; placed in; poked; prodded; put in; rubbed; slapped; smacked; smoothed over; smothered; stamped on; submerged; swept off; took; tripped over; twisted.

Descriptive Phrases

Her feet were smooth and supple, and he longed to feel the weight of them in his hands.

Pins and needles shot down her legs and made her feet tingle.

She was swept off her feet by this hunk of a man.

The little girl heard footsteps approaching and quickly leaped under the bed.

The man exposed his bare foot, it was dirty, and each nail yellowed with age.

29
Words and Phrases to Describe the Body

Root Words

body; lower body; upper body.

Adjectives

all-too-willing; amazing; arched back; aroused; bare; bronzed; brown; cold; dark; delectable; exquisite; felt sensitized; feminine; firm; frantic; glorious; gorgeous; hard; hot; imposing; jittery; lean; limp; lithe; little; luscious; lush; magnificent; masculine; mouth-watering; muscular; naked; olive-skinned; overheated; pale; perfect; petite; plump; powerful; rebellious; ripe; rolled; sensitive; silky; slim; stacked; sun-darkened; tanned; taut; tender; tiny; voluptuous; warm; well-formed.

Descriptive Combinations

electricity sparking in her body; every cell in his body; every muscle in her body tensed; hard, hot body; lean, powerful body; lithe, sun-darkened body; perfect, petite body; ridges and valleys of his body; superb shape of his body; the heart of her body.

Verbs – Things the Body Can Do

ached; ached for; became aware; begged for; bent down; blossomed;

burned; came alive with feeling; cascaded through; constricted; contorted; convulsed; curled; curved; displayed; drew into; exposed; felt hot; felt restless; felt ultra-sensitive; filled with; flushed; gave out; hardened; heat crept up; heated; heat ripped through; hurt; inspired; jittered; joined; laid; leaned to one side; lowered; perspiration filmed; perspired; pleasure coursed through; posed; pressed against; quickened; quivered; raised; reared up; rebelled against; relaxed; responded; retreated; revealed; sagged; seared; sensations moved through; settled; shifted; shivered; shiver slithered through; shook; showed off; shuddered; softened against; sprang to life; squirmed; steadied; stiffened; stirred; strained; stretched; surged; swayed; swung; tensed; tension coiled in; tension left; tightened; tightened around; tingled; trembled; tremor shook; turned; twisted; wanted; warmed; went limp; went rigid; went taut; went tense; yielded.

Verbs – Things That Can Be Done to the Body

abandoned hold on; belonged to; brushed; caressed; charted; claimed; covered; cradled; explored; eyes glued to; eyes roamed over; forced; gripped; hated; held; held close to; held tightly against; hugged; hypnotized by; kissed; latched onto; licked; lifted; loathed; loved; massaged; pressed against; ran hands over; rubbed; shuddered against; skimmed hands over; smoothed lotion onto; soothed; steadied; stoked; stole the breath from; supported; touched; trembled against; wanted.

Descriptive Phrases

Every muscle in her body tensed with expectation.

Her body quivered with a desire she'd never felt before.

Her whole body ached with longing.

Seeing him there across the room made her body tingle from head to toe.

The strange tingling sensation gripped her body like a vise.

30
Words and Phrases to Describe Skin

Root Words

flesh; skin.

Adjectives

aged; bare; bluish; bronzed; brown; bruised; calloused; clammy; cold; creamy; dark; dark-colored; dry; exposed; fair; fevered; flawless; flushed; freckled; gold; hair-roughened; hardened; heated; hot; inflamed; light-colored; lined; moist; olive; oversensitive; pale; patchy; perspiring; pink; ravaged; reddened; rough; satin; sensitive; sensitized; shiny; silken; silky; smooth; soft; spotty; sun-warmed; sunburnt / sunburned; supple; sweaty; tanned; taut; tender; warm; wet; white; worn; wrinkled.

Descriptive Combinations

creamy, smooth skin; golden skin tone; his skin hot against hers; pale creamy flesh; skin so soft and tender; skin to skin; velvet soft skin; warm, soft skin.

Verbs – Things Skin Can Do

blushed; carmined; chilled; crimsoned; displayed; exposed; flamed; flushed; flushed pink; goosebumps grew on; gooseflesh bloomed on;

hardened; heated; hurt; perspired; reddened; showed; stretched over; sweated; tightened; tingled; tingled with desire; warmed.

Verbs – Things That Can Be Done to Skin

breathed in; breathed on; breathed over; bruised; burrowed under; caressed; clung to; craved; cut into; felt; felt the heat of; flirted with; glanced at; hand explored; heated; lavished; licked; massaged; nails dug into; nipped; planted a kiss on; ran thumb gently over; reveled in; scraped; shot a glance at; skimmed over; smoothed over; stared at; stroked; studied; stung; sucked; teased; tempted by; thumb brushed; touched; wanted to feel; warmed; water lingered on; wet; yearned for.

Descriptive Phrases

Her cool breath fanned his sunburned skin.

His fingers gently caressed her sun-warmed skin.

His fingers tingled as they skimmed over her soft skin.

She could feel the heat of his skin against her own.

She pressed hot, open-mouth kisses to his hair-roughened skin.

PART II:
Describing Senses and Emotions

32
Senses

Words Describing Taste

acerbic; acidic; acrid; aftertaste; agreeable; alkaline; appetizing; astringent; bad; biting; bitter; bittersweet; bland; brackish; briny; burnt; buttery; cardboard; caustic; crap; crisp; delectable; delicious; dominating; dry; dulcet; fishy; flavorful; foul; fresh; fruity; full; full-bodied; gamy; gingery; good; gourmet; greasy; gross; gustatory; hearty; honey; hot; icy; juicy; lemony; lip-smacking; medicinal; mellow; melted; mild; mouth-watering; nice; nip; nutritious; nutty; okay; overripe; palatable; peppery; pickled; piquant; pleasing; powerful; prickly; pungent; rancid; rank; raw; relish; rich; ripe; rotten; saccharine; saline; salty; saporific; savory; scrumptious; seasoned; sec; sharp; sour; spicy; spoiled; stale; sticky; strong; succulent; sugary; sweet; syrupy; tangy; tart; tasteless; tasty; toothsome; treacly; uneven; unripe; vinegary; weak; wet; whet one's appetite; wooden; yum; yummy; zesty; zingy.

Words Describing Touch and Texture

abrasive; angular; arid; bald; ballooned; barbed; bendable; biting; blemished; blistered; bloated; blunt; boiling; bolstered; bouncy; breezy; bristly; broad; broken; bubbly; bulging; bulky; bumpy; burning; burnished; bushy; caked; carved; chafing; channeled; chapped; chilly; chipped; chunky; clammy; clean; coagulated; coarse; coated; cold; cool; corrugated; cottony; covered; cozy; cratered; creamy; crisp; crocheted; crooked; crunchy; cuddly; curly; cushioned; cut; cut into; cutting; damaged; damp; dank; deep; dehydrated; dense; dented; dirty; disfigured; distended; downy; drenched; dripping; dry; ductile; dull; durable; dusty; elastic; embossed; enameled; encrusted; engorged; engraved; etched; even; expanded; explode; fat; feathery; fiery; filmy; filthy; fine; finished; firm; fizzy; flaky;

flat; flattened; flawed; flawless; fleecy; fleshy; fluffy; fluted; foamy; fragile; freezing; fresh; frigid; frosty; frothy; furred; furry; fuzzy; gelatinous; glassy; glazed; glossy; gnarled; gooey; grainy; granular; grating; gravelly; greasy; grimy; gritty; grooved; grubby; grungy; gusty; hairy; hard; harsh; heated; honeycombed; hot; humid; hygienic; icy; ill-defined; immaculate; impenetrable; imperfect; imprinted; incised; incrusted; indented; inflated; inflexible; inlaid; inscribed; inset; ironed; irregular; itchy; ivory; jagged; jarring; jumbled; knitted; knobbed; knotted; layered; leathery; level; lined; loose; lukewarm; lumpy; lusterless; lustrous; malleable; marked; matted; mellifluous; melted; metallic; mild; moist; mosaic; mucky; mushy; muted; mutilated; neat; non-glossy; oily; orderly; ornamented; padded; parched; patterned; pebbly; perfect; piercing; pitted; plastic; pleated; pliable; pocked; pockmarked; pointed; pointy; polished; potholed; powdery; precise; prickly; printed; protected; puffed out; puffed up; puffy; pulpy; pure; ragged; raw; razor sharp; refined; ribbed; ridged; rigid; rocky; rough; rubbery; runny; rusted; rutted; sandy; sanitary; satiny; saturated; scalding; scaled; scaly; scarred; scorching; scored; scraped; scratched; scratchy; sculptured; searing; serrated; set in; shaggy; sharp; sharp-edged; sheen; sheer; shielded; shiny; silky; silky-smooth; sleek; slick; slight; slimy; slippery; slushy; smooth; smudged; snug; soaked; soapy; sodden; soft; soggy; soiled; solid; sopping; sound; sparkling; spiky; spiny; spongy; spotless; springy; steamy; steely; sterile; sticky; stiff; stinging; strong; stubbly; stuccoed; sweaty; sweltering; swollen; syrupy; tacky; tarnished; tender; tepid; tessellated; textured; thick; thin; thorny; tight; tiled; tingly; tough; tweedy; unadulterated; unbreakable; uncomfortable; uncompromising; unctuous; undulating; uneven; unsoiled; untainted; untarnished; unyielding; varnished; velvety; veneered; warm; waterlogged; wavy; waxy; well-defined; well-honed; wet; withered; woolly; wooly; woven; yielding.

Words Describing Sight

adequate; adorable; alert; alive; angled; angular; asleep; awake; aware; bad; beautiful; bent; big; billowy; black; blinding; blonde; blotchy; blue; blurry; branching; bright; brilliant; broad; brunette; bulky; carved; checkered; chubby; circled; circular; clean; cloudy; colorful; colossal; contoured; craggy; creepy; crinkled; crooked; crowded; crystalline; curved; cute; damp; dangerous; dark; dead; deep; dim; dirty; disorganized; distinct; dowdy; dull; elegant; encircled; enormous; evil; fancy; fashionable; fat; filthy; flat; flickering; fluffy; foggy; forked; fuzzy; gigantic; glamorous; gleaming; glistening; globular; glowing; good; graceful; grassy; green;

grotesque; hard; harrowing; haunting; hazardous; hazy; high; hollow; homely; horrible; huge; icy; immense; important; innocent; light; lithe; little; long; low; magenta; messy; misty; moist; mossy; motionless; muddy; murky; musky; musty; narrow; orange; organized; out of focus; overcast; painted; pale; patterned; peaceful; petite; pitch-black; portly; purple; quaint; radiant; rainy; rectangular; red; reddish; rippling; rocky; rotund; rusty; scary; serene; shadowy; shallow; sharp; shaved; sheer; shimmering; shiny; short; shrunken; skinny; slippery; small; snowy; soaring; soft; sparkling; spotless; spotty; square; steep; stormy; straight; strange; sunny; tacky; tall; tapering; terrifying; tranquil; translucent; twinkling; ugly; unfocused; unique; unsightly; unusual; vicious; violent; weird; wet; white; wide; wiry; wispy; withered; wizened; wooden; wrinkled; yellow.

Words Describing Sound

angelic; annoying; audible; babbled; banged; barked; bassy; bawled; beat; bedlam; bellowed; blared; blasted; blatant; bleated; blustered; boisterous; boomed; boomy; brassy; brawled; brayed; bubbled; bumped; burped; buzzed; cackled; cacophonous; caterwauled; cawed; chatted; chattered; cheeped; chimed; chirped; chortled; chuckled; clamored; clamorous; clangored; clapped; clashed; clattered; clear; clucked; commotion; cooed; crackled; crashed; creaked; croaked; crooned; crowed; crunched; cried; deafening; dinned; discordant; dissonant; disturbing; dripped; droned; drummed; ear-piercing; ear-splitting; earth-shattering; easy on the ears; echoing; euphonious; exclaimed; faint; fizzed; footsteps; full; gagged; gasped; gibberish; grating; ground; groaned; growled; gulped; gurgled; harmonious; harsh; havoc; hawed; high; high-pitched; hissed; hoarse; hollow; honked; hooted; howled; hubbub; hushed; husky; impetuous; inarticulate; inaudible; intemperate; jangled; jingled; keened; eerie; knocked; lapped; loud; low; low-pitched; mellifluous; melodic; melodious; mewed; moaned; mooed; muffled; mumbled; murmured; muttered; noisy; obstreperous; pandemonium; pealed; peeped; piercing; pinged; pitch; pleasant; plopped; poignant; popped; pounded; prattled; punishing; pure; purred; quiet; racket; rambunctious; rang; rapped; rasped; raspy; rattled; raucous; resonated; reverberated; rhythmic; ripped; roared; rowdy; rumbled; rumbustious; rustled; scratched; screamed; screeched; shouted; shrieked; shrill; shuddered; shuffled; sighed; silent; sang; sizzled; slammed; slapped; sloshed; slurped; smashed; snapped; snarled; sneezed; sniveled; snorted; sobbed; soft; sonorous; soothing; splashed; squalled; squawked; squeaked; squealed; squelched; staccato; stomped; strident; strummed; sweet; swished; tapped; tore; thudded; thumped; thunderous;

thunked; timbre; tinkled; trickled; tinny; tolled; tranquil; trill; trumpeted; tumult; tuneful; tuneless; twanged; twittered; unruly; uproarious; vehement; vociferous; voiceless; volume; wailed; warbled; whacked; wheezed; whimpered; whined; whispered; whistled; whooped; yapped; yelled; yelped; yodeled.

Words Describing Smell

acidic; acidy; acrid; alluring; antiseptic; aromatic; balmy; biting; bitter; briny; burning; burnt; calming; camphoric; captivating; charming; choking; citrusy; clean; comforting; corky; dainty; damp; dank; delectable; delicious; delightful; desirable; distinctive; earthy; enchanting; favorable; fetid; fishy; flagrant; flowery; foul; fragrant; fresh; fruity; funky; gamy; gaseous; heady; heavenly; heavy; high; laden; lemony; lovely; luscious; medicinal; metallic; mildewed; minty; moldy; musky; musty; nasty; noxious; odoriferous; odorless; odorous; peppery; perfumed; piney; pleasant; pleasing; powerful; pungent; putrid; rancid; redolent; reek; relaxing; rich; rose; rotten; salty; savory; scented; searing; sexy; sharp; sickly; skunky; smelly; smoky; soothing; sour; spicy; spoiled; stagnant; stale; stench; stinking; stinky; strong; stuffy; sulfuric; sweaty; sweet; tart; tempting; vinegary; welcoming; woody; yeasty.

32
Feelings

Feelings and Emotions

abandoned; absolved; abused; acceptance; accepting; accountable; accused; adamant; adequate; admiration; adoration; affected; affection; affectionate; afraid; aggravated; aggressive; agitated; agony; alert; almighty; alone; amazement; ambitious; ambivalent; amused; anger; angst; anguish; animated; animosity; annoyed; anticipation; anxious; apathetic; apologetic; appalled; appreciative; apprehensive; ardent; argumentative; aroused; ashamed; astonished; astounded; at ease; attacked; attraction; awe; awful; bad; baffled; beaten down; beautiful; betrayed; bewildered; bitchy; bitter; blamed; blessed; blissful; blue; boastful; bold; bored; bossed around; brave; breathless; bright; brokenhearted; brushed off; bubbly; burdened; calamitous; calm; camaraderie; capable; captivated; cautious; certain; certainty; challenged; charmed; cheated; cheerful; childish; clever; close; cocky; cold; collected; combative; comfortable; comforted; compassion; competitive; concerned; condemned; confident; conflicted; confused; considerate; conspicuous; contempt; content; controlled; courageous; cowardly; crafty; cranky; crazy; critical; criticized; cruelty; crummy; crushed; culpable; curious; cut down; cynical; daring; dark; deceitful; deceived; defeated; defensive; dehumanized; dejected; delighted; delirious; denial; depression; desire; desirous; despair; desperation; destructive; determined; detested; devastated; devoted; different; diffident; diminished; dirty; disappointment; disapproved of; disbelief; discontented; discouraged; disgusted; disheartened; dismal; dispirited; disrespected; distracted; distraught; distressed; disturbed; divided; dizzy; dominated; dopey; doubt; down; downcast; downtrodden; drawn toward; dread; dreadful; dreary; dubious; dynamic; eager; earnest; easy; ecstatic; elated; electrified; embarrassed; emotional; empathic; emptiness; enchanted; encouraged; energetic; enervated; engrossed; enigmatic; enjoyment; enlightened; enmity; enraged; enthralled; enthusiastic; envious; euphoric;

evil; exasperated; excited; exhausted; expectation; exuberant; falsely accused; fascinated; fawning; fearful; festive; flabbergasted; flirtatious; flustered; foolish; forced; fortunate; fragile; frantic; frazzled; free; friendly; frightened; frisky; frustrated; fulfilled; full; furious; gay; giddy; glad; gleeful; gloomy; good; goofy; grateful; gratified; gratitude; gray; great; greedy; grief; groovy; grouchy; grudging; guarded; guilty; gullible; happiness; harassed; hardy; hatred; heartbroken; heavenly; helpful; helpless; high; high and mighty; homesick; honored; hopeful; hopeless; horrible; horrified; hostile; humiliated; hungry; hurt; hyper; hysterical; ignored; impatience; important; imposed upon; impressed; imprisoned; impulsive; inadequate; indifference; indignation; infatuated; inferior; infuriated; inhibited; inner peace; innocent; inquisitive; insanity; insecure; insignificant; inspired; insulted; intent; interested; interrogated; in the wrong; intimidated; intrigued; invaded; invalidated; invidious; invisible; irate; irritable; irritated; isolated; jaded; jealous; joyous; jubilant; judged; jumpy; keen; kindness; kinky; labeled; lazy; lecherous; lectured to; left out; let-down; liberated; lied about; lied to; lively; loathsome; lonely; longing; lost; love; loved; lovesick; low; loyal; lucky; lustful; mad; manipulated; maudlin; mean; melancholic; mellow; merciful; merry; mildness; miserable; misled; misunderstood; mixed up; mocked; morbid; mourning; naughty; needed; needy; neglected; nervous; nice; nostalgia; nosy; nutty; obligated; obnoxious; obscene; obsessed; odd; offended; opposed; optimistic; out of control; outraged; over-controlled; over-protected; over-ruled; overjoyed; overwhelmed; pacified; pain; panicked; panicky; paralyzed; paranoia; parsimonious; passionate; pathetic; peaceful; persecuted; perturbed; pessimistic; petrified; phobic; pissed; pity; playful; pleasant; pleased; pleasure; possessive; powerless; precarious; pressed; pressured; pretty; pride; prim; prissy; proud; provocative; provoked; punished; put down; puzzled; quarrelsome; queer; quiet; rage; rapture; reassured; rebellious; receptive; refreshed; regret; reinforced; rejected; relaxed; reliable; relieved; reluctance; remorse; repentant; reprehensible; resentful; resignation; resolved; responsible; restless; restricted; reverent; rewarded; ridiculed; righteous; robbed; sadness; safe; sated; satisfied; scared; scorn; screwed up; secure; seething; selfish; sensitive; sensual; serene; servile; settled; sexy; shame; shamefaced; shamelessness; sheepish; shocked; shy; sick; silly; sincerity; sinful; skeptical; sleepy; smugness; sneaky; snoopy; solemn; somber; sorrow; sorry; spirited; spiteful; startled; stereotyped; stingy; strange; stressed; strong; stuffed; stunned; stupefied; stupid; submissive; suffering; suffocated; sunny; superior; sure; surprised; suspicious; sweet; sympathetic; talkative; teased; temperamental; tempted; tenacious; tender; tense; tentative; tenuous; terrible; terrified; terror; thankful; thirsty; threatened; thrilled; thwarted; tired; to blame; tormented;

torn; touched; tranquil; trapped; troubled; trust; turned off; turned on; ugly; uncared for; uncertainty; under-protected; underestimated; undernourished; understanding; uneasy; unhappy; unheard; unholy; unimportant; uninformed; unique; unkind; unknown; unloved; unsafe; unsettled; unsupported; untrusted; unwanted; upset; used; used-up; useless; valued; vehement; vengeful; vicious; villainous; vindictive; violated; violent; vital; vivacious; vulnerable; wanted; warm; wary; weary; weepy; whiny; wicked; wonder; wonderful; worn-out; worried; worthless; wounded; wrathful; wretched; wrong; yearned; zany; zesty.

Adjectives

ablaze; abounding; addictive; aggressive; agonizing; alert; alluring; amazing; animated; aromatic; aroused; arrogant; attractive; aware; beautiful; blushing; boiling; bright; brilliant; burning; calm; carefree; charming; cool; dashing; dazzling; deep; defiant; delicate; delicious; delightful; delirious; dramatic; eager; electric; enchanting; enthusiastic; erotic; ethereal; excited; exciting; exuberant; exultant; fervent; fervid; fierce; flawless; fluttering; frenzied; gentle; gleaming; glistening; gorgeous; graceful; greedy; heavenly; helpless; hypnotic; impassioned; impulsive; inflamed; knowing; learned; longing; magnificent; needing; passionate; petulant; possessive; powerful; receptive; romantic; scandalous; scintillating; stimulated; striking; tender; venomous; vigorous; wanting; weak; wild.

Verbs

anticipated; arose; attached; attacked; balanced; banged; bathed in; begged; beheld; bended; blew; boiled; bolted; bombarded; bounced; bound; breached; broke; built; buried; burned; burst; buzzed; carved; cast a spell; caught; caught up in; caused; challenged; charged; charted; chased; choked; circled; claimed; clamped; clung; coiled; collected; commanded; competed; connected; contained; contracted; controlled; coursed; covered; cracked; crackled; crashed; crawled; crossed; crushed; curled; curved; cut; defined; delighted; delivered; developed; disappeared; disarmed; displayed; dissected; divided; dove; dragged; drained; drew; dripped; dropped; drowned; drummed; dug; dwelled; electrified; endured; engulfed; ensnared; enveloped; escaped; excited; exhibited; expanded; exploded; extended; extracted; faded; fed; felt; filled up; flashed; fled; flew; flickered; floated; flooded; flowed; flowered; flung; folded; followed;

forced; formed; fought; found; froze; gathered; gazed; generated; glowed; glued; governed; grabbed; grated; groaned; ground; guarded; guided; hammered; handled; haunted; headed; healed; hid; hit; hooked; hovered; hugged; hummed; hung; hunted; hurried; ignited; imagined; increased; induced; initiated; injected; intensified; interfered with; interrupted; jammed; joined; jolted; jumped; kept; kicked; kissed; knitted; knocked; knotted; laid; landed; lasted; launched; leaped; led; licked; lifted; lit; loaded; locked; longed; loosened; loved; maintained; manipulated; married; matched; melted; mended; met; mined; mixed with; nailed; navigated; nested; numbed; obeyed; observed; obtained; offered; opened; ordered; oriented; overcame; overflowed; overtook; owned; packed; parted; passed; paused; peeled; penetrated; performed; picked; pierced; pinched; pinpointed; placed; planted; played; pleaded; pointed; possessed; poured; preserved; pressed; pricked; pulled; pulsed; pulse quickened; pumped; punctured; punished; pushed; raced; radiated; rained; raised; ran; ravished; realized; received; recognized; reduced; reflected; refused; reigned; relaxed; released; remained; removed; rendered; repeated; replaced; responded; robbed; rode; rolled; rose; rubbed; ruled; rushed; sailed; sat; saturated; scattered; scolded; scorched; scraped; screamed; sealed; searched; seeped; sensed; set ablaze; set aflame; set alight; set on fire; settled; shaved; shed; sheltered; shivered; shocked; shook; shot; shrunk; shut; sighed; sipped; sizzled; slid; slowed; smashed; soothed; sounded; sparked; sparkled; sped; spilled; split; spoke; sprayed; spread; sprouted; sprung; spun; squeezed; squirmed; stained; stared; started; steered; stimulated; stirred; stole; stood; stretched; stripped; stroked; struck; stuck; studied; stung; stunned; suggested; sung; supplied; supported; surrounded; suspended; swallowed; swam; swelled; swept; swirled; switched; swung; thundered; trapped; unfastened; unified; unlocked; used; vanished; visited; wailed; waited; wandered; wanted; warmed; washed; watched; wavered; weaved; wet; whined; whipped; whispered; winded; wiped; withdrew; wobbled; wore; worked; wound; wrapped; wrestled; wriggled; wrung; zipped; zoomed.

33
Facial Expressions

Adjectives

absent; acceptance; accepting; accomplished; affected; afflicted; aggravated; aggressive; agony; alluring; almost boyish; amused; angry; annoyed; anxious; apathetic; appalled; appealing; aroused; ashamed; awareness; awe; bamboozled; barely perceptible; bashful; beatific; benevolent; bewildered; bilious; bitchy; bittersweet; black; blank; bleak; blinking; blissful; blithe; bloodthirsty; bored; bouncy; boyish; bright; brooding; bug eyed; buzzed; calm; carefree; chagrined; cheeky; cheerful; cheerless; cherubic; chipper; choleric; cleverness; cocky; cold; comely; concentrated; confident; confused; contemptuous; contentment; cowardly; coy; cranky; crappy; crazy; crestfallen; crooked; crushed; cunning; curious; cynical; dark; daydreaming; deadpan; dejected; delighted; delirious; depressed; derisive; desire; despondent; determined; devastated; devious; dirty; disappointed; discomforted; discontent; discouraged; disgust; displeased; distracted; ditsy; doleful; dorky; dour; downcast; drained; dreamy; drunk; dumbfounded; easygoing; ecstatic; elated; encouraged; energetic; enraged; enthralled; entranced; envious; etched; evasive; excited; exhausted; expressionless; faint; famished; fantasizing; fatalistic; fatigued; fear; fierce; fixed; flabbergasted; flirty; frightened; frustrated; full; full of grief; furtive; gazing; geeky; giddy; giggly; glancing; glaring; glazed; gloomy; glowering; glowing; good; grateful; grave; grim; groggy; grumpy; guilty; happy; haughty; haunted; high; high-strung; hollow; hopeful; hopeless; horny; hostile; hot; hot-tempered; humiliated; humorless; hungry; hunted; hyper; ill-natured; immobile; impassive; impressed; indescribable; indifferent; indignant; inexpressive; infuriated; inquisitive; inscrutable; insolent; insulting; intent; intimidating; irate; irked; irritated; jealous; jeering; jubilant; knowing; lamentation; languid; lazy; leering; lethargic; lighthearted; listless; lit; lively; lonely; loved; lucid; lustful; mad; malevolent; malicious; maliciously playful; meaningful; melancholy; mellow; mental; mild; mischievous; mocking;

moody; morose; muted; mysterious; naughty; nerdy; nervous; nonchalant; numb; obstinate; okay; optimistic; pained; pain stricken; pallid; peaceful; peering; peeved; pessimistic; petulant; pissed off; pissy; pitying; playful; pleading; pleased; pouting; predator; preoccupied; prickly; questioning; quixotic; quizzical; radiant; recumbent; refreshed; rejected; rejuvenated; relaxed; relieved; reproachful; resentful; resistant; restless; roguish; rushed; sad; sadistic; sadness; sanguine; satisfied; scared; scornful; scowling; searching; serious; set; sexually suggestive; shamefaced; shocked; shy; sick; sickly; silly; slack-jawed; sleepy; sly; smart; snarling; sneering; snobby; somber; sour; staring; stealthy; stern; stolid; straight-faced; stressed; strong; stupid-looking; submissive; sulky; sullen; surly; surprised; suspicious; sweet; sympathetic; taunting; taut; tense; tepid; thankful; thoughtful; threatening; tight; tired; tormented; touched; twisted; unblinking; uncomfortable; unpleasant; unreadable; unwavering; urbane; vacant; veiled; vengeful; wan; wary; weak; weary; weird; wide eyed; wild eyed; wistful; withering; woeful; wolfish; worried; wrathful; wry; yearning.

Verbs

bawled; beamed; blinked; breathed; cackled; came alive; chortled; chuckled; contorted; cried; curled lip; dropped jaw; eyed; eyes narrowed; faded; flexed brow; flexed jaw; frowned; furrowed brow; gaped; gave a look; gawked; gazed; giggled; glanced; glared; glinted; gloated; glowed; glowered; goggled; grew dark; grimaced; grinned; jeered; jutted; knitted eyebrows; laughed; leered; let out a breath; lit up; looked; lowered; made a face; mocked; mouthed; peeked; peered; pinched brow; pouted; puckered lips; pulled a face; pursed lips; raised; raised eyebrows; rolled eyes; scanned; scowled; screamed; screwed up; scrunched up; set; sighed; sighted; smelled; smiled; smirked; snarled; sneered; sneezed; snorted; sobbed; spied; spotted; squawked; squished; squinted; strained; studied; stuttered; sucked in a breath; sulked; surveyed; swallowed; twisted; waned; watched; wept; winced; winked; wrinkled; yelled.

Descriptive Phrases

An annoyed expression briefly crossed his face.

He gave her a look of contempt.

He looked up at her with an expression of optimism.

Her expression shifted from bewilderment to agony.

His expression faded from coy to serious.

His face contorted with hatred and disgust.

She glanced over at him and saw a blank expression staring back.

She stared at him, her expression wary.

She turned up her nose at him, expressing her insolence.

She watched him, a brooding look on her face.

The look on his face pulled at her heartstrings.

PART III:
Describing Intimacy

34
Voice

Root Words

throat; voice.

Adjectives

accented; articulate; booming; burning; calculating; clear; cold; controlled; cynical; dark; deep; distant; echoey; edgy; emotionless; enticing; excited; faraway; fierce; fiery; flat; gloating; hard; harsh; hollow; husky; icy; inarticulate; inviting; lifeless; little; loving; luxurious; masculine; muffled; musical; muted; pained; primal; raw; rough; rusty; sensual; sexy; shaking; sharp; silken; silky; small; smooth; soft; stifled; strained; strong; sulky; sullen; sweet; tender; thin; tight; trembling; tuneful; uncontrollable; velvet; warm; weak; wobbly.

Descriptive Combinations

a strange note in his voice; burning sighs; convulsive gasps; cries of ecstasy; dark masculine voice; groans of delight; His voice was thick with emotion; made a low noise in his throat; raspy moan; small, tight voice; unnaturally flat voice.

Verbs

broke; burned; coaxed; countered; cracked; cried out; cut through; echoed; exchanged words; faltered; framed; gasped; gloated; groaned; ground out; grunted; lowered; moaned; mumbled; muttered; overflowed with emotion;

petered out; provoked; quivered; raised; rang; said; scolded; screamed; shook; sighed; stammered; stated; summoned; thickened; trembled; voiced; whispered.

Alternative Words For Said

accepted; accused; acknowledged; added; addressed; admitted; advertised; advised; affirmed; agonized; agreed; alleged; announced; answered; apologized; appealed; approved; argued; arranged; articulated; asked; asserted; asseverated; assumed; assured; averred; avowed; babbled; barked; bawled; beamed; beckoned; began; begged; bellowed; beseeched; bleated; blubbered; blurted; boasted; boomed; bossed; bragged; breathed; broached; broadcast; broke in; bubbled; bugged; bullied; burst out; cajoled; called; carped; cautioned; censured; chatted; chattered; cheered; chided; chimed in; choked; chortled; chorused; chuckled; circulated; claimed; clucked; coaxed; comforted; commanded; commented; complained; conceded; concluded; concurred; condemned; conferred; confessed; confided; confirmed; congratulated; consoled; contended; continued; convinced; corrected; coughed; cried; cried out; criticized; croaked; crooned; crowed; cursed; dared; decided; declared; defended; demanded; denied; denoted; described; dictated; disagreed; disclosed; disposed; disseminated; distributed; divulged; doubted; drawled; echoed; emitted; empathized; encouraged; ended; entreated; exacted; exclaimed; explained; exposed; faltered; finished; fretted; fumed; gasped; gave; gawped; gibed; giggled; glowered; got out; greeted; grieved; grinned; groaned; growled; grumbled; grunted; guessed; gulped; gurgled; handed on; hesitated; hinted; hissed; hollered; howled; hypothesized; imitated; imparted; implied; implored; importuned; inclined; indicated; informed; inquired; insisted; interjected; interrupted; invited; jabbered; jeered; jested; joked; justified; keened; lamented; laughed; leered; lied; lilted; lisped; made known; made public; maintained; marked; marveled; mentioned; mewled; mimicked; moaned; mocked; mourned; mumbled; murmured; mused; muttered; nagged; necessitated; nodded; noted; objected; observed; offered; ordered; panted; passed on; piped; pleaded; pointed out; pondered; postulated; praised; prayed; preached; premised; presented; presupposed; proclaimed; prodded; professed; proffered; promised; promulgated; proposed; protested; provoked; publicized; published; puled; purred; put forth; put in; put out; puzzled; quaked; quavered; queried; questioned; quipped; quivered; quizzed; quoted; raged; ranted; reasoned; reassured; recalled; reckoned; rejoiced; rejoined; related; released; remarked; remembered; reminded; remonstrated; repeated; replied; reported; reprimanded; requested; required; requisitioned; responded; retorted; revealed; roared; sang; sassed;

scoffed; scolded; screamed; seethed; sent on; settled; shared; shot; shouted; shrieked; shrilled; shrugged; shuddered; sighed; smiled; smirked; snapped; snarled; sneered; sneezed; snickered; sniffed; sniffled; sniveled; snorted; sobbed; solicited; sought; specified; speculated; spluttered; spoke; sputtered; squeaked; stammered; started; stated; stormed; stressed; stuttered; suggested; supposed; surmised; swore; taunted; teased; tempted; tested; testified; theorized; threatened; thundered; told; told off; touted; trailed off; transferred; transmitted; trembled; trilled; trumpeted; understood; urged; uttered; verified; vociferated; voiced; volunteered; vouched for; vowed; wailed; wanted; warned; went on; wept; wheedled; whimpered; whined; whispered; wondered; worried; yakked; yawned; yelled; yelped; yowled.

Descriptive Phrases

An eerie voice split the silence like a knife.

He seized her by the throat, stifling her screams.

She heard a strange note in his voice which made her question his true motives.

She pleaded for him to come back, her voice trembling.

The memory of his warm voice branded her heart with remorse.

35
Breathing

Adjectives

audible; bad; calming; controlled; cool; deep; fracturing; gritty; hard; harsh; heavy; hurried; jagged; jerky; light; long; low; measured; pent-up; quick; quiet; quivering; ragged; rapid; raspy; raw; rough; shaky; shallow; sharp; shuddering; silent; slow; slowly; soft; steady; stilted; strained; struggling; sudden; taut; unsteady; warm.

Descriptive Combinations

breath caught in her throat; breath died in her throat; breathed a sigh of relief; breathed in and out; breathed in sharply; breath of relief; deep, shuddering breath; her breath came in tiny pants; knocked the breath from his lungs; low, steady sound of breathing; out of breath; stole the breath from her; took her breath away; very deep breath.

Verbs

absorbed; blew out; breathed; breathed in; breathed out; caught; down neck; dragged in; drew; evaporated; exhaled; expelled; expired; faltered; fanned; fractured; gasped; gulped in; held; hissed; inhaled; insufflated; panted; paused; puffed; pulled in; quickened; ran out of; rasped; recovered; released; respired; rushed; sighed; stifled; stilted; stopped; struggled to take; sucked in; suffocated; swallowed; took; went out; wheezed.

Descriptive Phrases

He expelled his breath in a slow, steady hiss.

Her breath caught in her throat.

His delicate touch made her inhale sharply.

His thoughts were swimming making it nearly impossible to breathe.

She struggled to take a breath.

She sucked in several deep breaths to calm herself.

The truth of her deception knocked the breath out of his lungs.

36
Kissing

Root Words

caress; embrace; kiss; make out; osculate; pash; peck; smooch.

Adjectives

brash; brutal; carnal; chaste; close-mouthed; deep; defiant; demanding; devastating; drugging; dry; erotic; faint; farewell; fiery; French; gentle; good-night; goodbye; hard; harsh; heated; heavy; hot; huge; hungry; hurried; impulsive; intense; intimate; light; lingering; little; long; mind-numbing; molten; molten-hot; open-mouthed; passionate; possessive; punishing; quick; raw; reluctant; rough; rugged; scintillating; seductive; sensual; sensuous; shaky; sinful; sizzling; sloppy; slow; smoldering; soft; sweet; tender; tentative; thorough; tongue-thrusting; torrid; trembling; urgent; warm; wet.

Descriptive Combinations

claimed her lips; deep, sensual kiss; hot, tongue-thrusting kiss; memory of the kiss; passionate, scintillating kiss; soft, wet kiss; stole a kiss.

Verbs

began; bent over to; blew; brushed over; continued; deepened; demanded; drew into; dropped on; drowned in; dying to; gave; greeted with; interrupted; kissed; laid on; leaned in; liked; osculated; peppered with;

planted on; pressed to; ran over; received; replayed; showered; silenced with; skimmed; smoothed; snatched; started to; stole; stopped; stopped with; swooped in for; thought about; trailed over; tried to; wanted to.

Descriptive Phrases

He kissed her like she'd never been kissed before.

He kissed her softly on the lips.

He leaned in and kissed her forehead.

He moved his hands over the back of her neck, then kissed her lightly on her lips.

She kissed him with a passion which took his breath away.

She pressed a kiss to his tanned chest.

37
Sex

Words That Describe Touching

brushed; caressed; connected with; contacted; cuddled; embraced; felt; flicked; fondled; grazed; hugged; nestled; nuzzled; patted; petted; scraped; shaved; skimmed; smoothed; snuggled; squeezed; stroked; swept; tickled; touched.

Words That Describe an Orgasm

aromatic; blasted; body thrummed; brink; burst; burst of pleasure; came; clenched; climaxed; crescendo; crested; desire; ejaculation; electric; erotic; exhilarating; exploded; feeling; fiery; frenzy; heat; heavenly; hot; impulse; intense; intimate; intoxicating; jolted; joy; liquid; lost control; nerve-endings fired; orgasmed; passionate; peak; penetrated; pleasurable; primal; rapture; reached the brink; released; relish; rose; rushed; satisfaction; sensation; shook; shot; shuddered; spark; spasmed; squeezed; squirted; swelled; swept away; thunderous; tingled; uncontrollable; warmth; warm wave; wave; waves of pleasure; wet; zenith.

Made in the USA
Monee, IL
07 July 2020